Southern Grace

WHERE EVERY STORY HOLDS A BLESSING

CHARLES E. CRAVEY

IN HIS STEPS PUBLISHING

All scripture is from the King James Version of the Holy Bible.

ISBN: 978-1-58535-101-5 (Paperback)

ISBN: 978-1-58535-102-2 (Hardcover)

ISBN: 978-1-58535-103-9 (EPUB)

Library of Congress Catalog Number: 2025910342

Published in the United States of America by:

In His Steps Publishing

DISCLAIMER: All persons mentioned in this book are fictional.

Contents

Introduction

In the gathering of these stories, I've come to understand that grace isn't just a word we say before supper—it's the thread that stitches together the fabric of Southern life. It's found in the way morning light catches the courthouse dome in Dahlonega, in how neighbors still check on neighbors after storms, and in the gentle wisdom passed down through generations like family recipes written on flour-dusted index cards.

These tales came to me like gifts: some whispered from rocking chairs on wraparound porches, others shared over coffee in small-town diners, and many discovered along back roads where Georgia's heart beats strongest. They're stories of people who understand that life's richest moments often come wrapped in ordinary packages, that true wealth is measured in relationships rather than dollars, and that sometimes the greatest acts of grace happen in the quietest ways.

SOUTHERN GRACE is more than a collection of stories—it's a testimony to a way of life that values front porch conversations over social media posts, which believes in the power of second chances, and that knows tomorrow's promises often depend on yesterday's wisdom. Each tale here is a reminder that in the South, grace isn't just something we talk about—it's something we live.

As you turn these pages, I invite you to slow down to Southern time, to let these stories settle in your soul like evening dew on morning glory vines.

For in the end, grace isn't found in grand gestures or mighty deeds—it's discovered in the small moments that make life large with meaning.

Welcome to SOUTHERN GRACE. Pull up a chair. Pour a glass of sweet tea. Let's share some stories that remind us why we call this blessed corner of earth home.

Charles E. Cravey, May 2025

1

"Ain't No Sunshine"

A Southern Story of Loss and Light

THE MORNING SUN SPILLED across Sarah Mitchell's empty porch swing, making the chains gleam like silver tears. Thomas stood in the doorway of their Valdosta home, watching that empty swing sway slightly in the Georgia breeze, remembering how she'd loved to sit there in the evening light, humming soft and low.

Forty-three years they'd shared that porch, watched their children grow, welcomed grandchildren, weathered storms both real and metaphorical. Now the swing moved without her, and the sunshine seemed to mock the darkness in his heart.

Miss Ruby from next door brought over a casserole, like southern neighbors do. "The sun still shines, Thomas," she whispered, patting his hand. "Sarah would want you to feel it."

But the world had lost its light when Sarah left it. The azaleas she'd tended bloomed pink and defiant. The mockingbirds still sang their morning songs, but everything seemed dimmer, as if the world itself missed her gentle presence.

When Light Leaves

Charles E. Cravey

The porch swing sways in morning air,

Where once she sat with silver hair.

Through empty days and lonely nights,

The world has lost its sweetest light.

The flowers bloom, the birds still sing,

Yet something's gone from everything.

The sun will rise, will set again,

But shadows linger deep within.

For love, once lost, leaves darkness deep,

Where memories sweet their vigil keeps.

Yet somewhere past the grief and pain,

Her light will help me shine again.

Reflection on Loss and Light

In the South, we measure grief in casseroles and covered dishes, in neighbors stopping by, in empty porch swings that still move in the breeze. Loss dims our world, makes shadows where once there was light, turns familiar places into landscapes of memory.

But southern grief carries its own grace—in the way communities gather, in the muted presence of those who understand that sometimes silence speaks louder than words, in the gentle reminder that even the darkest night eventually yields to dawn.

Because sometimes it's the deepest darkness that teaches us most about light.

2

The Heartbeat of America

A Chevy Man's Story

JIMMY PARKER'S CHEVROLET DEALERSHIP had stood on the corner of Main Street in Jesup, Georgia, since 1956. The showroom windows still gleamed like his daddy had taught him, and that bowtie emblem still caught the morning sun just right. Three generations of Parkers had sold more than cars here—they'd sold pieces of the American Dream, one set of keys at a time.

He remembered when the "Heartbeat of America" campaign first rolled out in '86, how perfectly it had captured something about Chevrolet, about Georgia, about America itself. The way his grandfather used to say, "Son, we ain't just selling cars—we're selling stories waiting to happen."

Today, as Jimmy walked past the '57 Bel Air he kept pristine in the showroom—his daddy's first car, now a shrine to memory—he thought about all the first cars, family vehicles, and dream machines that had rolled through these doors. Each one carrying hopes, each one part of someone's story.

"You know what makes a Chevy special?" he'd tell young buyers, running his hand along a fresh paint job. "It's not just the machine—it's the memories it'll help you make."

The Bowtie's Promise

Charles E. Cravey

Chrome gleams bright in Georgia sun,

Where dreams and drives become as one.

Through years that pass like highway miles,

Each Chevy carries hopes and smiles.

From father's first to son's own ride,

These bonds of steel run deep with pride.

The heartbeat strong, the stories true,

In Chevrolet's own gold and blue.

For some sell cars, while others know—

They're selling dreams that help souls grow.

Through every mile, through every day,

America's heart beats Chevrolet.

Reflection on America's Heartbeat

In the South, a car dealership is more than a business—it's a community landmark, a place where milestones are marked by new keys and fresh starts. The "Heartbeat of America" wasn't just a slogan; it was a truth written in chrome and steel, in family traditions and Saturday morning washes in driveways across Georgia.

These showrooms hold more than vehicles—they hold the stories of first dates and family road trips, of bringing babies home and sending kids to college, of dreams achieved and promises kept. Because in the South, we understand that a car isn't just transportation—it's a vessel for memories, a carrier of traditions, a way to keep the heartbeat of America strong and steady.

Because some rhythms run deeper than engines, some traditions shine brighter than chrome.

3

Tickled Pink

THERE AIN'T MUCH THAT can't be said better with a good ol' Southern expression. And when folks say they're "tickled pink," it's more than just being pleased—it's the kind of joy that bubbles up from your toes, spreads through your ribs, and plants a smile so wide it could stretch across a cotton field.

The first time I ever heard the phrase, it spilled out of Granny Cooper's mouth like sweet tea from a mason jar. We'd just pulled up to her creaking old porch, our dusty station wagon packed tight with kids, dogs, and Aunt Ruth's famous ambrosia. Granny Cooper bustled out to meet us, her apron smudged with flour and her cheeks already the color of peony blooms. "Well, I'm just tickled pink to see y'all!" she squealed, her laugh ricocheting through the hot summer air.

Granny Cooper didn't need to explain it—I could see what it meant in the way her arms flew open and the way her voice danced like sunlight on water. "Tickled pink" wasn't simply happy. It was joy so pure it made you feel like the entire world was exactly right, just for a moment.

It's the way your heart swells when the first azaleas burst into bloom after a gray winter, or when you spot a rainbow arcing over a pecan grove after a hard rain. It's the pride in whipping up a pie crust from scratch that Mama swears could give store-bought a run for its money. It's catching fireflies at dusk and watching their glow paint the air with magic.

Granny Cooper used to say, "Happiness is a color, darlin'—and when it paints you pink, you know it's special." That's the thing about the South: emotions here have flavors and textures, colors, and smells. "Tickled Pink" smells like peach cobbler fresh from the oven. It feels like the rough weave of a rocking chair cushion under your hands as you laugh with cousins. It lingers like the faint hum of a fiddle at a summer barn dance.

And once you've been tickled pink, you never forget the shade of it.

The Color of Joy
(A Southern-style poem)

Charles E. Cravey

When Granny smiled, the world turned bright.
Her laugh a song, her heart alight.
"Tickled pink," she'd always say,
As joy came dancing through the day.

The wind sang sweet through pine and oak.
The porch swing creaked, and the fireflies woke.
The kitchen smelled of sugar and spice.
Life's small treasures, rich and nice.

It's in the blooms, the sun-warmed air,
The way love lingers everywhere.
Its pie crusts golden, sunsets wide.
It's holding kin and time beside.

Oh, tickled pink, a gentle hue,
A color rare, a feeling true.
It stains the heart like summer's dye,
And paints the soul where mem'ries lie.

Southern Reflection

This speaks to the very soul of Southern wisdom. There's something here that captures what we in the South have always known - that the deepest truths often come wrapped in the simplest packages, like blackberries in a gingham cloth.

This piece weaves together what philosophers might call phenomenology (the lived experience of being) with what we down here just call "knowing in your bones." When Granny Cooper talks about happiness being a color, she's touching on something profound that formal philosophy often misses - the way our emotions are deeply embodied, tied to our senses and our stories.

I've linked "tickled pink" to the physical world—the peach cobbler's aroma, the rough texture of a rocking chair, the glow of fireflies - that's pure Southern epistemology right there. We understand truth through experience, through the senses, and through relationships. It's what philosopher

Maurice Merleau-Ponty tried to explain in fancy French terms, but my Granny Cooper said it better with a flour-dusted apron and an open heart.

We've found the universal in the particular. Each specific detail (the creaking porch swing, the pine and oak) opens up into something larger about joy, memory, and human connection. It's reminiscent of how Walker Percy wrote about the South - finding meaning not in abstract concepts but in the concrete details of lived experience.

This piece isn't just about being happy - it's about the way joy becomes real through community, through shared experience, and through the physical world. That's a profound philosophical statement about the nature of human experience and meaning, delivered with the grace of a screen door closing softly on a summer evening.

4

A Passion for Trees

IN THE SOUTH, TREES aren't just part of the landscape; they're part of the soul. They've stood watch through centuries of change, their branches stretching out like arms wide open, ready to offer shade, solace, and stories to anyone willing to listen.

Take the live oak, draped in Spanish moss like a grand dame showing off her finery. Beneath its shade, generations have gathered—children playing tag, elders swapping tales, and lovers carving their initials into the bark. A good shade tree isn't just respite from the heat; it's a sanctuary, a place where time slows and memories are made.

The pines are different—straight-backed and steady, whispering secrets in the breeze. The sound of their needles rustling is like a hymn, soft and steady, a reminder that peace can be found in the quiet moments. And then there are the magnolias, with their blossoms so bold they seem to demand attention. The fragrance is thick and sweet, clinging to humid afternoons and lingering in the folds of memory.

But beyond their beauty lies the redeeming quality of timber—the backbone of Southern survival and industry. Timber isn't just wood; it's homes built strong enough to withstand storms, bridges connecting communities, and fires kindled to warm cold nights. It's the craft of carpenters

and the dream of builders, turning nature's gift into something endur-
ing, something with purpose.

We don't just revere trees for what they give us; we love them for what
they are—steadfast and enduring, rooted yet reaching. Their seasons
mirror our own lives: growth in spring, flourishing in summer, letting
go in autumn, and resting in winter. To love a tree is to understand the
rhythm of the earth, to feel the pulse of something timeless and true.

The Song of the Trees
(A Southern-style poem)

Charles E. Cravey

The oak bows low, its moss held high,
A sentinel beneath the sky.
Its shade has kissed the brow of kings,
And cradled dreams where time still sings.

The pine stands straight, its whispers deep,
Through dusk and dawn, its vigil keeps.
Its wood a gift, its scent a prayer,
A quiet soul that soothes the air.

The magnolia blooms in bold display.
Its beauty is proud; its fragrance stays.

A queen of scent, a feast for eyes,
Its petals soft as summer skies.

Oh, timber tall, with strength and grace,
You build our homes; you shape our space.
Through fire and storm, through need and strife,
You give us warmth; you gift us life.

The trees, they speak in subtle tones.
Of earth's embrace, of roots and stones.
Their song resounds through fields and streams.
A Southern heart in leafy dreams.

5

Multi-Symptom Relief

BACK IN THE HOLLERS and hills of the South, medicine didn't come in shiny bottles from the corner drugstore. It was brewed, steeped, wrapped, and rubbed—a concoction of tradition, necessity, and a pinch of daring. At the heart of it all was moonshine, that fiery elixir that warmed your throat and your soul, doubling as medicine long before it was something to toast with.

They called it "white lightning," but to Granny Cravey, it was "miracle water." She'd keep a jar tucked away on the pantry shelf, hidden between sacks of flour and sugar. "Good for what ails ya," she'd say, sloshing a bit into her cast-iron skillet to sterilize it before dressing a wound. Burn your hand on the stove? Moonshine. Scratch from a bramble? Moonshine. It stung like the devil but cleaned better than anything you could buy for a nickel.

When winter rolled in and the coughing started—deep and rattling, the kind that shook the walls—Granny would whip up her famous cough remedy. A little moonshine, a squeeze of lemon, and a dollop of honey stirred together in a chipped mug. "Sip it slow," she'd say, as she set it steaming on the table. "The shine will chase off the chill, and the honey'll make it go down easy."

But moonshine wasn't the only weapon in Granny's arsenal. Poultices were a staple in her toolkit, too. For bee stings and spider bites, she'd mash up tobacco leaves and press them against the skin, muttering under her breath about how nature took care of its own. For aches and pains, there was a poultice of boiled onions, wrapped in an old dishtowel and tied snug around the sore spot. And if your belly was giving you trouble, a hot water bottle and a handful of peppermint leaves would fix you right up.

Even the land itself seemed to conspire in the name of healing. A sprig of rosemary tucked under the pillow for a headache. Epsom salts scooped into a tin bucket for aching feet. The bark of a willow tree brewed into a tea for fever—though Granny always said she preferred the moonshine "because it makes you feel better even before it starts working."

Medicine in the South wasn't just about fixing what was broken—it was about care, about paying attention to the rhythms of the body and the land, and about leaning into what you had and making it enough. Moonshine and poultices weren't just cures; they were a testament to resilience, ingenuity, and the belief that healing starts with what's already around you.

The Remedy's Charm
(A Southern-style poem)

Charles E. Cravey

A jar of shine, a sprig of thyme,
A poultice wrapped, a cure in time.
The hills provide, the old ways teach,
That healing lies in what we reach.

A scratch, a burn, a cough held tight,
The shine will warm the coldest night.
A leaf, a root, a brew so steeped,
The body mended, the spirit reaped.

Granny's voice, her steady hand,
Her knowledge is drawn from timeless land.
The willow bends, the fields provide,
And moonshine flows where aches reside.

Oh, Southern charm, oh, wisdom near,
A remedy for every fear.
The past still hums in jars and leaves.
In homes where care and love believe.

6

The Quiet Resolve of Clitus Walker

CLITUS WALKER, WHOSE NAME was as humble as the soil he tilled, found his days stitched together by sweat and solitude. He lived among those shadows cast by the Southside's rusting fences and sagging roofs, and the whispers of society weighed heavy like the warm Georgia air. Many considered Clitus a boy whose fate the crumbling tenement houses had sealed, but Clitus harbored dreams shimmering like sunlight through the cracks.

Each evening after work at Mr. Sexton's sprawling farm, Clitus would sit by the worn edge of the river, his hands still aching from the weight of watermelons and corn. His mind, however, drifted far from Harmony Creek. He saw the bright banners of a circus, heard the clash of war drums in far-off lands, and imagined the icy cliffs of Everest biting against the resolve of his spirit. The cool river breeze whispered to him that life's weight need not break his back nor his will.

(inspired by Harper Lee's wisdom):
"A man can still dream, even when he ain't got a penny to his name."

These words lingered in the back of Clitus's mind whenever he faced the biting remarks of the townsfolk. The whispers of his supposed "slowness" and the notion that he'd never be more than a farmhand could not touch the muted fire he carried within. His teacher's tales of distant lands were seeds sown in him, though unseen by the doubters.

Scripture Reflection:
"Do not despise these small beginnings, for the Lord rejoices to see the work begin."–Zechariah 4:10

Clitus found solace in the church's worn pews, where someone had painted this verse above the pulpit. It reminded him that even if his journey felt bound to the soil of Georgia, it could still bear fruit unknown.

Philosophical Ending:
The years passed, and Clitus remained in Harmony Creek, tethered to the rhythm of the farm and the pulse of the Southside community. To some, his dreams seemed squandered—but Clitus knew better. With every quiet act of resilience, every morning spent under the blazing sun, and every evening spent dreaming by the river, he carved out a dignity that no man could deny. He realized that a man's worth is determined not by the extent of his travels but by the unwavering courage he displays in facing his life. In this way, Clitus rose, not above, but *through* the narrow-eyed judgment of society.

> The soil grips tight, the roots dig deep,
> Yet dreams shall climb where spirits leap.
> What binds the hands cannot bind the heart.
> From humble ends, great lives can start.
>
> – Charles E. Cravey

7

The Wandering Pages

"The world is a book and those who do not travel read only one page." St. Augustine.

Ella had spent most of her life within the walls of her small town. The streets were her chapters, familiar and unchanging, the seasons her rhythm. Yet, deep within, a yearning stirred—a muted voice whispering that there was more to the story.

When she inherited her grandmother's weathered suitcase, it felt like an invitation. Inside, she discovered a collection of postcards from distant lands—the Eiffel Tower, the Serengeti, the Great Wall—all sent from strangers her grandmother had met during her travels. Scribbled on the back of each postcard were fragments of wisdom: *"To walk under Parisian lights is to see poetry take form." "A lion's gaze in Africa teaches humility."*

Ella realized that her life was not a finished story—it was barely the first page. Her suitcase became her companion, her ticket to discovery. In Istanbul, she marveled at the layered history of the Hagia Sophia; in Kyoto, cherry blossoms painted the air with fleeting beauty. Every new place revealed a different chapter, expanding her perspective, filling her heart with wonder and questions.

As she traveled, she understood Augustine's wisdom. To read only one page was to accept a narrow view, to leave the world's complexity unexplored. Every journey was a step toward understanding not only the world but also herself—a weaving together of landscapes, cultures, and stories into the tapestry of her existence.

Travel, in its essence, is an act of vulnerability and connection. It beckons us to step outside our comfort zones and embrace the unfamiliar. Augustine's metaphor challenges us to see life not as a stationary existence but as a dynamic process—a journey through chapters yet unwritten.

The "pages" of the world are not merely geographical; they are cultural, emotional, and existential. Every destination is an encounter with diversity, a confrontation with the unknown. But perhaps the most profound revelation of travel is that it teaches us about the universality of human experience—we may speak different tongues, but we share the same dreams, fears, and aspirations.

Through travel, we realize the vastness of possibility and the limitations of remaining within a single narrative. The act of exploration becomes a lesson in humility and wonder, reminding us that no matter how far we go, we are always students of life's boundless text.

The Wandering Pages

Charles E. Cravey

The world unfolds, a book immense,
Its words in skies and seas commence.

Each chapter, a land; each line, a face.
Each moment, a truth in time's embrace.

To walk new paths, to sail unknown seas,
Is to learn the rhythm of whispered pleas,
For the story we write with footsteps bold,
Is richer than treasures we ever hold.

A mountain's echo, a desert's song,
The pages call, and we belong.
Not bound by borders, nor shackled by fear,
Each chapter awaits its wisdom near.

So, take the pen, let journeys flow,
Through cities vast and valleys low.
For life's great tale, in wonder spun,
Is read by those who dare the sun.

As Ella's grandmother had once reminded her, "The suitcase is small, but its possibilities are infinite." Indeed, travel is more than movement—it's transformation. It's opening the book of life and allowing every chapter to enrich your soul.

So let us be travelers, seekers of wisdom, and readers of all the pages the world offers. For in the end, it is not the destinations we conquer but the horizons we expand.

8

To Conquer Oneself

"It is not the mountain we conquer, but ourselves." Sir Edmund Hillary.

As the first rays of dawn kissed the summit, Sarah tightened the straps of her worn backpack. The mountain loomed ahead, its jagged peaks cutting into the soft hues of the sky. A lifetime of preparation had led her here, yet her heart thundered with doubt.

Each step up the treacherous path was a battle—not against the terrain, but against the voice in her mind whispering: "You'll never make it."

Years ago, Sarah had been told she wasn't strong enough. Not strong enough to withstand the storm of life, not strong enough to scale anything as daunting as this. She had carried those words like stones, heavy and unyielding. But now, here she was.

As she ascended, memories surfaced like mist in the cold. Her father's stern advice, her coach's dismissive laugh, the weight of her own hesitation. Every slip of her boot on the loose rocks felt like facing her fears head-on.

Finally, with trembling hands and burning lungs, she reached the summit. She stood on top of the world, but as she gazed around, she realized something. The mountain hadn't been her enemy—it had been her ally all along, forcing her to confront and overcome her own self-doubt.

With a muted smile, Sarah whispered, "It wasn't about the summit. It was about the climb."

As Sarah ascended, she pondered the notion of conquest. Was reaching the summit truly an act of domination? Or was it an acceptance of her place within something larger—an acknowledgment of nature's indifference and her own impermanence?

The mountain, ancient and unyielding, whispered silent truths as she climbed. It was a reminder that humanity's achievements, though glorious, are fleeting. It asked her to consider: What is victory, if not the ability to rise above fear and embrace the struggle?

Sarah realized the climb was not a battle against an external force but a journey inward. The jagged rocks and biting wind were reflections of her own uncertainty, her desire to prove she could stand tall against life's adversities.

At the summit, she felt no triumph, no surge of conquest. Instead, there was peace—a stillness born of understanding. She had not conquered the mountain, for it did not need conquering. In truth, Sarah had conquered herself.

To Conquer Oneself

Charles E. Cravey

The mountain whispers, timeless and true,
A challenge not to the sky, but to you.
Its peaks do not hunger for triumph or praise.
They stand as a mirror to life's winding maze.

Each step, a question; each breath, a test.
Do you battle the world or your heart's unrest?
For conquest is fleeting, a moment's delight,
But victory within births an eternal light.

The winds, they howl with wisdom untamed.
The cliffs bear witness; each stone proclaimed,
"Rise, seeker of courage, from valleys low,
For strength blooms where the brave dare to go."

The summit, a throne, adorned by the sky,
Yet the climb holds the truth where answers lie.
So, ascend, not to conquer the vast or the steep,
But to awaken the depths where your soul may sleep.

For the true mountain lies within, concealed.
Awaiting the strength of a soul revealed.

As Sarah descended the mountain, the world below stretched out before her, vast and unbroken. The triumph was not a flag planted on a summit but a quiet strength carried in her chest. The journey had shown her that every peak, whether of Earth or spirit, was not an end but a beginning—an invitation to keep climbing, forever seeking, forever growing.

For in conquering herself, she had uncovered the boundless horizon of what it truly meant to be alive.

9

When the Cows Come Home

A Tale of Southern Time

When the Cows Come Home—A Tale of Southern Time

Every evening, just as the sun started painting the sky in peach and purple hues, Old Man Turner's dairy cows would make their slow procession home. Down the dirt road they'd come, their shadows stretching long across Miller County soil, moving with that unhurried grace that seemed to say time itself was merely a suggestion.

Folks in these parts had long since stopped using clocks to mark the evening hour. "I'll be there when the cows come home," they'd say, and everyone knew exactly what that meant. It wasn't just about time—it was about rhythm, about the natural order of things, about the way life moved in the deep South.

Young Billy Matthews would often sit on his grandpa's fence, watching that daily parade. "Why don't they ever get lost?" he'd ask, and his grandpa would smile, chewing on a piece of wheat straw.

"Son," he'd say, "some things just know where they belong. Ain't about thinking—it's about remembering."

The Evening Procession

Charles E. Cravey

Down dusty roads as day grows dim,

They amble home in evening's hymn.

Each hoof print marks the passing day,

While shadows dance in fading grey.

No hurry here, no rush to be,

Just ancient rhythms, wild and free.

Through summer heat and autumn gold,

They know the way, like stories old.

For time runs sweet in southern air,

Where patience grows without a care.

And wisdom lives in simple things,

Like knowing what each evening brings.

Reflection on Southern Time

In the South, we measure time differently—not by the tight constraints of minutes and hours, but by the natural rhythms that govern life." When the cows come home" isn't just a saying; it's a philosophy, a reminder that some things can't be rushed, shouldn't be hurried.

These daily rituals—the slow procession of cattle, the gathering dusk, the muted settling of day into night—teach us something profound about patience, about belonging, about the wisdom of knowing that everything happens in its own perfect time.

Because some clocks don't tick, they moo.

10

Broken Promises

A SOUTHERN TALE OF REDEMPTION

THE OLD HAWKINS PLACE sat empty now, its once-proud columns graying like forgotten promises. The peeling paint and sagging porch told a story familiar to many in Burke County—of dreams handed down, of expectations as heavy as the August air, of generations trying to keep promises made in different times.

James Hawkins stood in the overgrown driveway, keys heavy in his pocket. He'd promised his daddy he'd keep the family farm going, just as his daddy had promised his grandfather. But drought years, changing markets, and modern realities had worn those promises thin as old cotton sheets.

"Sometimes," his mama had told him before she passed, "keeping one promise means breaking another. The trick is knowing which ones matter most."

Now, watching his own son playing in the yard of their new suburban home across town, James understood. He'd broken his promise to the past to keep a promise to the future. The land would be sold, but his children would have opportunities his grandfather never dreamed of.

The Weight of Words

Charles E. Cravey

Promises fall like autumn leaves,

Some float away on evening's breeze.

While others sink into the ground,

Where roots of change can still be found.

Through years that stretch like cotton rows,

Some truths take time to decompose.

The weight of words from long ago,

Can bend us more than we might know.

Yet wisdom comes in learning when

To let some promises begin

Their gentle fall to yesterday,

So new ones have their chance to stay.

Reflection on Promise and Change

In the South, promises carry weight—they're currency traded across generations, obligations passed down like family Bibles. We learn early that a person's word should be as solid as Georgia granite, as dependable as summer heat.

But life teaches harder lessons: that sometimes love means letting go, that holding too tightly to yesterday's promises can strangle tomorrow's possibilities. The true measure of honor isn't in never breaking a promise—it's in knowing which ones to keep, which ones to lay gently down, and how to forgive ourselves when circumstances force our hands.

Because sometimes the most faithful thing we can do is change.

11

Charleston's King Street

WHERE TIME STROLLS

THE MORNING SUN CATCHES the wrought-iron balconies just so, casting lace-like shadows across centuries-old brick. King Street awakens slowly, deliberately, like a Southern belle preparing for her debut. From Broad Street to Spring, each block tells its own story—of merchants and mansions, of war and renewal, of a city that refuses to surrender its grace to time.

Miss Eleanor Davies had walked this street for seven decades, watching it transform yet somehow stay eternally itself. Her grandfather's antique shop still stood at Number 158, though now it sold designer handbags. She remembered when the sidewalks were quiet, before the haute couture boutiques and farm-to-table restaurants made King Street the crown jewel of Charleston's renaissance.

"The street adapts," she'd tell her granddaughter, "But it never forgets. Listen closely—you can still hear the clip-clop of horse hooves on cobblestones beneath the modern bustle."

Each storefront was a chapter: Croghan's Jewel Box, still sparkling after a century; the old Kress building wearing its art deco pride; College of Charleston students hurrying past windows where their great-grandparents once window-shopped.

The King's Promenade

Charles E. Cravey

Where iron lace meets morning light,

And history walks in modern sight,

The King still holds his royal way,

Through changes time makes every day.

Past windows filled with fashions new,

Where old brick wears a modern hue,

The street maintains its measured grace.

In every step, in every face.

For some streets lead just anywhere.

While King Street holds time's thoroughfare.

Through war and peace, through then and now,

Charleston's heart still takes its bow.

Reflection on Charleston's Eternal Grace

In Charleston, preservation isn't about freezing time—it's about letting it flow while keeping the essence intact. King Street embodies this philosophy perfectly, embracing progress while honoring its past. The old and new dance together here, each step measured by the rhythm of southern tradition.

The street reminds us that elegance isn't about perfection—it's about adaptation with grace. From antebellum glory through post-war struggles to modern renaissance, King Street has remained Charleston's backbone, its showcase, its beating heart.

Because some streets don't just connect places. They connect centuries.

12

A Peaceful Paradise for the Soul
A MEDITATION ON SACRED GROUND

THE OLD CAMP MEETING arbor at Indian Springs stood silent in the morning mist, its weathered beams holding a century of prayers. Pine straw cushioned footsteps as early risers made their way to the wooden benches, just as their grandparents and great-grandparents had done. Here, beneath these timbers, heaven seemed just a whisper away.

Sarah Matthews touched the rough-hewn post where her grandmother once leaned during evening services, feeling the smoothness worn by generations of hands. The same hymns still floated through the Georgia pines each summer, "Amazing Grace" and "Sweet Hour of Prayer" mingling with birdsong and cicada chorus.

The family cabins—"tents" as they were still called from the days when they really were canvas—stood in their neat rows, some dating back to the 1890s. Simple board-and-batten structures that held more memories than furniture. No air conditioning, just tall windows and screen doors that let God's breath move through.

"This is where peace lives," her grandfather used to say. "Where the world slows down enough to let your soul catch up."

Sacred Ground

Charles E. Cravey

Where pine trees pray in morning light,

And faith still walks through sacred night,

The old arbor stands in grace,

Time-worn beams in holy space.

Through summer heat and evening song,

Where prayers rise soft and praise lifts strong,

The Spirit moves in gentle ways,

Through simple truths of simpler days.

For some seek peace in marble halls,

While here, between these wooden walls,

A paradise of soul remains,

Where heaven touches earth again.

Reflection on Finding Paradise

In the South, paradise isn't always grand or gilded—sometimes it's found in sawdust floors and wooden benches, in the space between verses of an old hymn, in the quiet moments before dawn when only prayer breaks the silence.

These camp meetings remind us that sacred spaces aren't built of stone and stained glass alone. They're built of memories and meditation, of generations joining hands across time, of traditions that anchor our souls in an ever-changing world.

Because sometimes paradise isn't a place you find—it's a peace you inherit.

13

Southern Nature's Chorus

A Symphony in Green and Gold

Just before dawn, when the world held its breath between night and day, the South's great symphony began. First chair went to the whip-poor-will, its plaintive call rolling across the misty hollows. Then came the mourning doves, their soft coos like prayers rising through the pines, followed by the mockingbirds with their endless medley of borrowed songs.

Down by Carter's Creek, bullfrogs added their bass notes, while cicadas built their crescendo in the heavy afternoon air. The wind through Georgia pines provided the strings section, a constant whisper-song that spoke of ancient things.

Old Doc Wilson, who'd spent sixty years listening to this chorus from his wraparound porch in Screven County, called it "God's own radio station." He knew every movement by heart—from the spring peepers' dawn reveille to the cricket's evening vespers.

"City folks pay good money for what they call 'sound therapy,'" he'd say, rocking slowly as a chorus of tree frogs began their evening song. "But out here, we just call it listening."

Nature's Hymnal

Charles E. Cravey

The whip-poor-will begins the day,

While morning glories have their say.

Through buzzing bee and butterfly,

Each creature lifts its voice on high.

The pines they whisper, old and true,

While hawks cry circles in the blue.

Through noon heat's lazy katydid,

To evening's cricket chorus bid.

For music lives in southern air,

In every wing and flower fair.

This symphony of wild and free,

Nature's perfect harmony.

Reflection on Heaven's Orchestra

In the South, we understand that silence isn't really silent—it's filled with a thousand voices speaking in leaves and wings, in water over stones, and in wind through Spanish moss. This chorus reminds us we're part of something larger, something wild and wonderful that sings whether or not we're listening.

Nature's music teaches us patience, teaches us to slow down and tune our ears to frequencies that can't be captured on any recording. It reminds us that the finest concerts aren't in grand halls but in humble places—a farm pond at sunset, a pine forest at dawn, a summer garden humming with bees.

Because sometimes the sweetest music isn't made by man at all—it's the song creation has been singing since the beginning of time.

14

Finding Forgiveness, the Southern Way
A Tale of Grace and Grits

MISS SARAH BETH HENDERSON had held onto that grudge like it was her mama's prize cast-iron skillet—fourteen years of not speaking to her sister Ruby over words spoken harshly at their daddy's funeral. Fourteen years of separate pews at First Baptist, of missed birthdays and holidays, of neighbors having to set two different coffee times to visit with each sister.

It was the smell of her mama's chocolate pound cake that finally broke the wall between them. Ruby had baked one for the church social, using their mama's recipe, the one Sarah Beth thought only she had. When that familiar sweetness drifted across the fellowship hall, something inside Sarah Beth crumbled faster than that cake's crispy edges.

"Mama would've hated this," she whispered to herself, watching her sister serve slices with that same graceful wrist-turn their mother had used. Before she knew what she was doing, Sarah Beth was standing at Ruby's elbow.

"Looks just like Mama's," she said softly.

Ruby's hands trembled slightly as she cut another slice. "Got one in the car," she replied, "Still warm. Was gonna bring it by your house after."

The Weight of Grace

Charles E. Cravey

Grudges weigh like summer heat.

While grace flows sweet as tea.

Through years of silence, hurt held tight,

Till love finds a way to set things right.

Some wounds need time to soften slow,

Like biscuits need time just to grow.

But Southern hearts, though stubbornly strong,

Know grace takes time to right a wrong.

For healing comes in its own way,

Through pound cake shared on God's good day.

When pride bows down to memories sweet,

And sisters find their way to meet.

Reflection on Southern Forgiveness

In the South, forgiveness often comes wrapped in butter and sugar, served on grandmother's china with a side of humility. We understand that some hurts run deeper than others, that healing takes its own sweet time, like sorghum syrup flowing slow and steady.

Our way of forgiveness isn't about forgetting—it's about making room at the table anyway. It's about understanding that family bonds, like pepper sauce in a vinegar bottle, only get stronger with time, even when they sting a little.

Because sometimes the hardest words—"I'm sorry" and "I forgive you"—taste sweetest when served with a slice of pound cake and a memory of Mama's love.

15

Finding Forgiveness: Part Two

THE CASSEROLE BRIGADE

WHEN FRANK PATTERSON'S YOUNGEST boy got himself into trouble over in Metter—the kind that made headlines in the Candler County Chronicle—the first sign of grace arrived in a 9x13 Pyrex dish. Miss Martha from the Methodist Women's Circle brought her famous chicken and dressing, still warm from the oven.

"Sometimes," she said, setting it on Frank's kitchen counter, "the Good Lord works through green bean casseroles and sweet potato pies."

They came in waves after that. The Baptist ladies brought their hash brown casseroles, the Presbyterian women arrived with pound cakes, and even the Church of God folks showed up with their signature banana puddings. Each dish came with the same message: "We're still here. We still care. This too shall pass."

Frank's wife Mary hadn't been to church since the news broke—couldn't bear the weight of those eyes, those whispers. But the food kept coming, Sunday after Sunday, until Mary finally understood sometimes forgiveness smells like mac and cheese and feels like the weight of a covered dish.

The Healing Dishes

Charles E. Cravey

Grace comes covered, wrapped in foil,

Born of loving hands that toil.

Through casseroles and comfort food,

Speaks a truth long understood.

When words fail and hearts are sore,

Love slides gently through the door.

In dishes brought with quiet care,

Forgiveness seasons evening air.

For Southern grace knows how to feed

Both body and the soul in need.

Till shame dissolves in chicken broth,

And mercy tastes like butter cloth.

Reflection on Community Grace

In the South, we understand that forgiveness isn't just a word—it's an action, often served in disposable aluminum pans with careful instructions for reheating. When judgment could come easily, we choose instead to bring sustenance, to feed both body and soul.

Our mothers taught us that a well-timed casserole can speak louder than words, that banana pudding can bridge gaps that arguments only widen. We learned that sometimes the weight of covered dishes brought by caring hands lightens the heaviest burdens.

Because true grace isn't about deserving—it's about delivering love in whatever form it takes, even if that form is a hash brown casserole with extra cheese on top.

16

Finding Forgiveness: Part Three
THE FRONT PORCH TRIBUNAL

OLD MISS BEATRICE JOHNSON'S front porch had been South Georgia's unofficial court of reconciliation for nearly four decades. That white wooden swing and those ladder-back rocking chairs had seen more feuds resolved than the county courthouse. Her secret weapon? Sweet tea so sugary it could make even the bitterest hearts soften.

When the Anderson brothers stopped speaking over their daddy's tractor, Miss Beatrice invited them both to "help her move some flowerpots." They arrived at different times but somehow ended up on that porch together, two grown men shifting uncomfortably while Miss Beatrice poured tea and talked about their mama's prize-winning dahlias.

"Y'all know," she said, settling into her creaking rocker, "your daddy used to say a tractor ain't worth much compared to having somebody to work it with." Then she just sat there, letting the evening cicadas preach their sermon while that sweet tea did its work.

The Porch of Peace

Charles E. Cravey

Where wooden slats meet evening air,

And rockers creak like whispered prayer,

The ministry of front porch grace

Brings healing to this sacred space.

Through ceiling fans and mason jars,

Past pride that bends but leaves no scars,

The wisdom of the ages flows

In tea so sweet it helps hearts grow.

For somewhere 'tween the day and night,

When fireflies begin their flight,

Old wrongs dissolve like sugar sweet,

Where porch swing wisdom can't be beat.

Reflection on Porch Diplomacy

In the South, we know people negotiate some of the most powerful peace treaties not in marble halls but on wooden porches. There's something about the rhythm of a porch swing, the hypnotic spin of ceiling fans, and the shared ritual of sipping sweet tea that helps soften the hardest hearts.

Our front porches serve as confessionals, counseling offices, and courts of appeal—places where the gentle art of listening can heal wounds that shouting only makes worse. We understand that sometimes the best mediator is a silent rocker and the patience to let evening settle in.

Because true reconciliation, like the best sweet tea, can't be rushed—it needs time to steep in the warmth of Southern grace.

17

MountainTime

A Tale from the North Georgia Hills

Up in Rabun Gap, where the mountains hold their secrets close and the morning fog clings to the valleys like a grandmother's quilt, time moves different. That's what old Hank Welborn always said, tending his apple trees on the same steep hillside his grandfather had terraced by hand back in 1923.

The tourists who came up from Atlanta to see the fall colors would rush past in their shiny SUVs, hunting beauty like it was something you could chase. But Hank knew better. He'd learned from sixty years of mountain living that beauty comes to those who know how to wait—like the way the sun takes its time painting the hillsides gold and crimson each October, or how the best apples need that first frost kiss to reach their sweetest.

"Mountain folks," he'd tell his grandchildren, "We don't fight time—we flow with it, like water finding its way down to the valley." His orchard proved it: Grimes Golden, Arkansas Black, and Yellow June apples, each variety ripening in its own season, none of them hurrying, none of them late.

Mountain Wisdom

Charles E. Cravey

Where peaks rise proud through morning mist,

And time flows slow as morning's kiss,

The mountains keep their ancient ways,

Through changing seasons, changing days.

Past apple trees on terraced ground,

Where wisdom comes without a sound,

The heights teach those who choose to stay

That beauty can't be rushed away.

For mountain time runs deep and slow,

Like springs that feed the streams below.

Through patience learned on sacred ground,

Where peace in stillness can be found.

Reflection on Mountain Grace

In North Georgia's mountains, we learn a different kind of wisdom—one that can't be rushed or bought, only absorbed through years of watching the mist rise and the seasons turn. These ancient hills teach us that some things are worth waiting for, that the sweetest rewards often come to those who understand nature's rhythms.

The mountains remind us that strength isn't always about standing firm—sometimes it's about knowing how to bend with the weather, how to put down roots deep enough to hold through any storm, how to grow slowly but grow true.

Because some lessons can only be learned at altitude, where the air is thin and time is thick with meaning.

18

The Clayton Cliffs

WHERE HEAVEN TOUCHES GEORGIA

THE MORNING SUN CAUGHT the face of Rabun Bald just right, turning the granite cliffs to fire above Clayton's sleepy streets. Down at the Flour Sack Café, breakfast regulars watched the show through plate glass windows while Martha Jean served up cathead biscuits and her famous apple butter.

"That mountain," Doc Henderson would say between sips of black coffee, "she puts on a different dress every morning." And he was right—sometimes wrapped in clouds like a bride's veil, sometimes stark against a winter sky, sometimes softened by summer's green cloak.

The new folks, who'd built their fancy mountain homes with floor-to-ceiling windows called it their "million-dollar view." But the old-timers knew better. Some things couldn't be bought or sold—like the way the hawks rode the thermals in lazy circles, or how the first snow of winter would dust the cliffs like powdered sugar on one of Martha Jean's biscuits.

Every local had their own mountain story: first kisses at Black Rock overlook, family picnics at Rabun Beach, or that time lightning danced across the ridgeline like God's own light show.

The Mountain's Song

Charles E. Cravey

Where granite meets the morning light,

And mist unveils the sacred height,

The ancient cliffs their stories tell,

In language time has taught them well.

Through seasons' dance of sun and shade,

Past memories that never fade,

The mountain keeps her quiet way,

New stories born with each new day.

For some see rock and weathered stone,

While others hear the mountain's tone—

A song of earth and sky entwined,

Where heaven's touch leaves grace behind.

Reflection on Mountain Majesty

In North Georgia, we understand that mountains aren't just features on a map—they're characters in our daily story, silent guardians of our traditions, keepers of our secrets. They remind us that some things stand unchanged while the world rushes by below.

These cliffs teach us about permanence in a world of change, about standing firm while remaining beautiful, and about the difference between existing and enduring. They show us that true majesty doesn't need to announce itself—it simply needs to be.

Because some landmarks don't just mark land—they mark souls.

19

The Chattooga's Song

WILD WATERS OF NORTH GEORGIA

WHERE THE CHATTOOGA RIVER cuts through the mountains, there's a sound that can't be captured in recordings—a wild symphony of water over rock, of history rushing downstream, of something ancient and untamed. Section Four, they call it, where the river shows its teeth in rapids with names like Bull Sluice and Five Falls.

Old River Joe, who'd guided rafts down these waters for forty years, knew every whisper and roar. "This ain't just any river," he'd tell his nervous passengers as they put in near Earl's Ford. "This is where the mountains tell their stories—if you've got the courage to listen."

The morning fog would lift off the water like spirits rising, revealing the rhododendron-choked banks and towering hemlocks that had seen centuries of water flow past. Sometimes, in the muted stretches between rapids, you could hear the river's secrets—tales of Cherokee fishers, of moonshine runners, of endless seasons of rain and drought.

"People come here thinking they're gonna conquer the river," River Joe would say, watching the sun dance on the rapids. "They leave understanding that the best you can hope for is to dance with it awhile."

The River's Dance

Charles E. Cravey

Where waters wild meet mountain stone,

Each rapid speaks in thunder-tone.

Through gorges deep and forests high,

The Chattooga sings her lullaby.

Past rocky shoals and quiet pools,

Where nature keeps her ancient rules,

The river flows in timeless grace,

Teaching those who seek this place.

For some streams trickle, some streams play,

But mountain waters know their way—

Through centuries of rain and shine,

Dancing down their grand design.

Reflection on Wild Waters

In these North Georgia mountains, the Chattooga reminds us that some things shouldn't be tamed, that there's profound beauty in what remains wild and free. The river teaches us about power and humility, about knowing when to fight the current and when to flow with it.

These waters carry more than just fallen leaves and mountain rain—they carry lessons about life itself: that the path of least resistance isn't always the best path, that beauty often lives where danger dwells, that some journeys are best measured in heartbeats rather than miles.

Because some rivers don't just flow through the land—they flow through our souls.

20

Dahlonega's Gold

WHERE DREAMS STILL GLITTER

THEY SAY THERE'S STILL gold in these hills—not just the kind that sparked America's first gold rush in 1829, but the kind that shines in autumn sunsets over the square, gleams in the windows of century-old storefronts, and glows in the hearts of those who call this mountain town home.

The old Price Building stands proud on the square, its brick facade telling tales of prospectors and dreamers who once traded dust and nuggets at its counters. Now it houses tourists sipping wine from local vineyards, but if you press your hand against those old walls, you can almost feel the fever of those gold rush days.

Professor Jim McKay, teaching geology at North Georgia College for thirty years, would take his students panning in the Yahoola Creek every fall. "Gold's not just about what's in the pan," he'd say, watching their eager faces as they swirled their sediment. "It's about what the searching does to your soul."

Even now, after all these years, locals still tell stories of their granddaddies finding nuggets after heavy rains, of secret spots up in the hills where the creek beds still sparkle, of dreams as bright as any metal.

Mountain Gold

Charles E. Cravey

Where autumn gilds the mountain air,

And dreams still linger everywhere,

The hills hold secrets, old and bright,

That glitter in the fading light.

Through streams that tumble, clear and cold,

Past stories of that rush for gold,

The mountains keep their treasures near,

For those with hearts to persevere.

For some seek wealth in yellow dust,

While others find what time can't rust—

The riches in a sunset's glow,

Or friendship's gold in hearts that know.

Reflection on Lasting Treasure

In Dahlonega, we understand that true gold isn't always what glitters in the pan. Sometimes it's found in the way morning light hits the courthouse dome, in the laughter of students crossing the university drill field, or in the taste of muscadines fresh from mountain vines.

These hills remind us that the richest veins aren't always under-ground—they run through our communities, our histories, and our shared dreams. They teach us that some treasures can't be measured in ounces or carats, but in moments and memories.

Because some wealth isn't counted—it's lived.

21

Suches – The Valley Above the Clouds
WHERE TIME TAKES A DEEP BREATH

UP HERE AT 2,792 feet, where Georgia touches heaven's front porch, Suches sleeps like a cat in mountain sunshine. The locals call it "The Valley Above the Clouds," watching morning mist pool in the hollows below while their little piece of paradise floats like an island in the sky.

Woody Gap School—the smallest public school in Georgia—stands as the heart of this unincorporated community, where everyone knows not just your name, but your grandparents' stories. Here, class sizes are measured in single digits, and the school's bell can be heard clear across the valley, marking time like it has since the days when Arthur Woody, the famous forest ranger, walked these hills.

Old Tom Pritchett, tending his garden near the intersection of Highway 60 and 180, remembers when the Appalachian Trail hikers first started coming through Woody Gap. "They come up here looking for wilderness," he'd say, pushing seeds into spring soil, "but what they find is something rarer—they find quiet."

The kind of quiet that makes your soul settle, which lets you hear tree frogs singing backup to whip-poor-wills, which reminds you some places stay exactly as God made them.

Mountain Whispers

Charles E. Cravey

Where morning mist meets mountain air,

And silence speaks like morning prayer,

The valley holds its treasured peace,

Where time itself finds sweet release.

Through seasons soft and mountain ways,

Past hurried world and busy days,

This haven floats on clouds of grace,

Where heaven claims its resting place.

For some towns rush to meet the new,

While Suches keeps its mountain view—

A place where souls can learn to rest,

In nature's high and holy nest.

Reflection on Sacred Stillness

In Suches, we understand growth does not always measure that progress. Sometimes it's measured by what remains unchanged—the way sunlight filters through ancient hemlocks, how neighbors still check on neighbors, how children can safely walk to a school smaller than most city classrooms.

These mountains teach us that some places are sanctuaries, where the modern world's chaos dissolves in mountain laurel blooms and wood smoke. These mountains show us we might count true wealth in summer lightning bugs, winter's first snow, and the luxury of unhurried conversations on country store porches.

Because some towns don't need to be big to be important—they just need to be authentic.

22

Lake Burton's Secrets

WHERE MOUNTAINS MEET WATER

AT DAYBREAK, WHEN MIST rises off Lake Burton like spirits of the valley folk who once called this land home, you can almost see the ghost of the old town beneath the waters. Before Georgia Power flooded the valley in 1919, Burton was a thriving mountain community—now it sleeps beneath one of the clearest lakes in the South, its stories rippling up through 2,775 acres of mountain-cradled water.

Charlie MacAllister, whose grandfather helped build the dam, keeps his wooden pontoon boat in a slip near LaPrade's Marina. "Every drought," he says, steering toward Timpson Cove, "the lake gives up a little more history—an old foundation stone, a piece of farm equipment, sometimes even a memory we thought was lost."

The lake holds different stories for different folks. For the summer people in their million-dollar homes, it's a slice of mountain paradise. For the old families, it's where their roots run deeper than the water. For the fishing guides, it's where spotted bass hide in underwater forests that once were hillside groves.

At sunset, when the mountains paint themselves purple on the water's surface, even the loudest boat engines can't drown out the whispers of what lies beneath.

The Drowning Valley

Charles E. Cravey

Where mountain waters deep and still,

Hold secrets of each buried hill,

The lake keeps time in liquid grace,

While memories float up through space.

Past sunken farms and covered dreams,

Through crystal depths where history gleams,

The stories rise like morning mist,

Of valley life, the waters kissed.

For some lakes spring from nature's hand,

While others claim what once was land—

Yet both hold truth in waters deep,

Where mountain spirits choose to sleep.

Reflection on Liquid Memory

In North Georgia, we know that progress often comes with a price, that sometimes yesterday must be sacrificed for tomorrow's needs. But Lake Burton teaches us that what's lost isn't always gone—it just takes a different form.

These waters remind us that change, like the lake itself, can reflect beauty even while covering scars. They show us how a community can reinvent itself while honoring what came before, how loss can transform into legacy.

Because some places don't just hold water—they hold time itself.

23

The 'Hooch

SACRED WATERS OF THE SOUTH

LONG BEFORE THEY CALLED it the Chattahoochee—before Helen became Bavaria, before Lake Lanier drowned the red dirt farms—the Cherokee knew these waters as Chat-to-ho-che, "marked rocks river," where ancient petroglyphs told stories in stone. Today, from its birthplace near Jack's Knob in Union County, through the mountain valleys and down past Atlanta's sprawl, the river still writes its own story in water.

Up in Helen, where the river's still young and playful, summer tubers float past like human confetti, their laughter mixing with the water's song. But old-timers like Ray Thomason remember when these waters meant more than recreation. "This river," he'd say from his porch overlooking the shoals, "was our highway, our power plant, our life's blood. Still is, if you think about it right."

Down at Sautee Creek's confluence, where the morning fog creates river spirits that dance on the water, you can sometimes hear the echoes of mill wheels that once turned by these banks. The 'Hooch powered their dreams, ground their corn, washed their gold, carried their timber—a liquid thread stitching together mountain communities.

River's Memory

Charles E. Cravey

From mountain spring to valley deep,

Where ancient waters secrets keep,

The 'Hooch flows down through time and tale,

Past marked rocks and misty vale.

Through Helen's streets and mountain ways,

Past golden dreams of bygone days,

The river writes in liquid hand.

Its story on this sacred land.

For some, they see just a stream that flows.

While others hear what history knows—

A song of people, place, and time,

Set to water's endless rhyme.

Reflection on Living Waters

In Georgia, we understand that rivers aren't just waterways—they're time-keepers, storytellers, and life-givers. The Chattahoochee reminds us that some things remain constant even as they constantly change, flowing ever onward while staying forever home.

These waters teach us about persistence, about finding our way around obstacles, and about the strength that comes from following our true nature. They show us how to be both powerful and gentle, how to shape the land while being shaped by it.

Because some rivers don't just flow through landscapes—they flow through generations, carrying yesterday's memories to tomorrow's dreams.

24

Land of the Trembling Earth
TALES FROM THE OKEFENOKEE

WHERE THE SOLID GROUND of Georgia dissolves into mystery, the Okefenokee spreads its dark waters across 438,000 acres of legend and lore. The Seminole named it well—"Land of the Trembling Earth"—where islands of peat float like living rafts, where ancient cypress trees wear Spanish moss like gray beards of wisdom.

Billy Thrift, third-generation swamp guide out of Folkston, knows every water trail and gator hole from Stephen C. Foster State Park to the Suwannee River outflow. "This ain't just any swamp," he'd say, poling his wooden boat through water black as coffee. "This here's a living book of Genesis, still writing itself every day."

In the early morning, when mist rises off the tea-colored water and wood storks wade like ghosts among the lily pads, you can almost hear the whispers of the old swampers—the Chesser family, the Lee family, those hardy souls who carved out lives in this water-bound wilderness. Their stories still echo across the prairie-like expanses where carnivorous plants dance in the breeze and sandhill cranes trumpet their ancient calls.

Trembling Earth's Song

Charles E. Cravey

Where cypress knees pierce blackened seas,

And gators glide through whispered breeze,

The swamp holds secrets, dark and deep.

Where trembling earth its watch does keep.

Through watery trails and floating ground,

Past ancient things not lost but found,

The stories rise like morning mist.

From waters time has blessed and kissed.

For some see darkness, deep and wild,

While others find a beauty styled

By God's own hand in water-light,

Where day dissolves in swamp-song night.

Reflection on Wilderness Wisdom

In the Okefenokee, we learn that solid ground is sometimes an illusion, that life finds a way to thrive in the most unlikely places. The swamp teaches us that beauty doesn't always wear pretty faces—sometimes it comes with scales and teeth, with mud and mystery.

These waters remind us that some places should remain wild, should stay beyond our ability to tame or understand completely. They show us that wilderness isn't just about untouched nature—it's about keeping alive the part of our souls that remembers how to be untamed.

Because some lands don't just tremble—they make our hearts tremble too, with wonder and with wild respect.

25

Water Trails

GEORGIA'S LIQUID HIGHWAYS

FROM THE ALTAMAHA'S BROAD shoulders to the Toccoa's mountain dance, Georgia's water trails weave stories through our state like blue silk threads through a family quilt. Each one carries its own voice—the Broad River's gentle murmur, the Flint's limestone whispers, the Ocmulgee's ancient song.

Down on the Altamaha River Water Trail, where Spanish moss drips silver in moonlight, kayakers paddle past sites where 18th-century sailing ships once anchored. "This river's been a highway longer than Georgia's been a state," says Mark Williams, whose family has fished these waters for five generations. "The Altamaha doesn't just flow through Georgia—it flows through time."

Up on the Etowah River Water Trail, paddlers glide past Native American fish weirs—V-shaped rock formations still pointing their secrets upstream after a thousand years. Each bend reveals another chapter: Civil War crossing points, abandoned gold mines, ancient fish traps that still work their quiet magic.

The Toccoa River Canoe Trail meanders through the Chattahoochee National Forest like a blue ribbon dropped from heaven, offering fourteen miles of mountain-wrapped serenity. Here, between the shoals, trout fishers stand like herons, their lines dancing with the current's rhythm.

River Roads

Charles E. Cravey

Through mountain vale and coastal plain,

Past cypress grove and sugar cane,

The water trails their stories tell,

In language time has taught them well.

Down liquid paths where history flows,

Through channels every paddler knows,

These ancient highways still persist,

Where water meets the morning mist.

For some roads run through field and town,

While others flow both up and down—

These trails that nature carved with care,

Through Georgia's heart beyond compare.

Reflection on Flowing Paths

In Georgia, we understand that rivers are our oldest highways, our most faithful storytellers. They remind us that every journey doesn't need a paved road—sometimes the best paths are carved by water, marked by the seasons, and measured in paddle strokes.

These water trails teach us that the journey matters more than the destination, that some stories can only be heard when we slow down to river time. They show us how to read the water's language, written in ripples and eddies, in sandbars and shoals.

Because some trails don't leave footprints—they leave ripples that echo through generations.

26

Summerville

A SLICE OF SOUTHERN GRACE

UP IN CHATTOOGA COUNTY, where the valley meets the mountains' embrace, Summerville dozes in Georgia sunshine like a contented cat on a wide front porch. The courthouse clock still marks time in town square chimes, just as it has since 1909, its copper dome weathered green with dignity.

The old Couey House stands sentinel in Dowdy Park, its hand-hewn logs from the 1840s telling tales of settlers who first called this valley home. Next door, the restored depot and turntable remind folks of when the railroad was king, when the Chattanooga, Rome & Columbus line brought the world to Summerville's doorstep.

Miss Eleanor at the Paradise Gardens Foundation loves to tell visitors how folk artist Howard Finster put Summerville on the world's artistic map. "This town," she says, arranging flowers by the visitor center, "has always known how to dream bigger than its size."

Down at the local diner, where breakfast conversations flow as smoothly as the coffee, old-timers remember when the textile mills hummed day and night, when Trion's cotton fields stretched white to the horizon, and when summer evenings meant ice cream socials at the Baptist church.

Valley's Embrace

Charles E. Cravey

Where mountain shadows gently fall,

And courthouse chimes still welcome all.

This valley town its peace maintains,

While modern rushing elsewhere reigns.

Through seasons sweet and years gone by,

Past cotton fields 'neath Georgia sky,

The stories linger, soft and true,

In morning mist and evening dew.

For some towns race to change their ways.

While others treasure slower days—

Like Summerville, whose gentle pace

Still measures time with Southern grace.

Reflection on Small Town Wisdom

In Summerville, we understand that progress doesn't always mean change, that some things are worth preserving—like front porch conversations, Sunday dinner traditions, and the way neighbors still check on neighbors after storms.

These streets remind us that community isn't built on size or speed, but on the strength of shared stories, on the bonds forged through generations of shared lives. They teach us that sometimes the richest lives are lived in the quietest places.

Because some towns don't need to be big to be significant—they just need to be authentic.

27

Good Lord Willing and the Creek Don't Rise

A Southern Promise

Every true Southerner knows this saying isn't just a farewell—it's a philosophy wrapped in a promise, seasoned with wisdom passed down like a family recipe. The phrase comes from days when creeks were the difference between making it to church on Sunday or staying home to pray, when rising waters could cut off communities as surely as a locked gate.

Miss Eunice Mason, who'd taught Sunday School at First Baptist for over forty years, always ended her prayers with these words. "It's not about doubting," she'd explain to her young charges. "It's about remembering who's really in charge of tomorrow."

When Hurricane Sally flooded Black Creek back in '22, old Mr. Johnson stood on his porch watching the water rise toward his steps. "Good Lord's willing it to rain," he said calmly to the rescue workers, "and sure enough, that creek did rise. Reckon He's got His reasons."

It's more than just weather wisdom—it's a humble acknowledgment that our plans, no matter how careful, always rest in bigger hands. From barn raisings to baptisms, from weddings to funerals, Southerners have seasoned their promises with this gentle reminder of life's uncertainty.

The Creek's Wisdom

Charles E. Cravey

Some promises we make with pride,

While others take the Lord as guide.

Through waters deep and waters wide,

We learn to let His will decide.

Past floods that rise and rains that fall,

Through nature's wild and wakening call,

These words of wisdom still ring true,

In humble hearts both old and new.

For some see just a saying old,

While others find there wisdom's gold—

That plans are best when gently laid,

With faith in how the path is made.

Reflection on Southern Grace

In the South, we understand that the best plans are written in pencil and sealed with prayer. This saying teaches us about humility, about the wisdom of leaving room for God's will in our daily plans, and about accepting that sometimes the creek rises for reasons beyond our understanding.

These words remind us that true wisdom lies not in controlling tomorrow but in facing it with grace and faith. They teach us that sometimes the most powerful thing we can do is acknowledge our own powerlessness.

Because some phrases don't just speak truth—they carry the weight of generations who learned that truth the hard way.

28

"Well, Bless Your Heart!"

THE SOUTH'S SWEETEST SWORD

IN THE SOUTH, THESE three little words can mean anything from genuine sympathy to the genteel equivalent of a verbal smackdown—all delivered with a smile as sweet as Vidalia onions and wrapped in enough sugar to make a honeybee blush.

Miss Charlotte DuBois, who'd reigned over the Garden Club for thirty years, was an artist with the phrase. She could make "bless your heart" dance on the edge between kindness and criticism like a hummingbird between blooms. When young Mrs. Patterson showed up at the spring flower show with plastic flowers, Miss Charlotte just tilted her head, smiled like sunrise on magnolias, and said, "Well, bless your heart, sugar. How... creative."

Down at Mae's Beauty Shop, where the real news of Habersham County got filtered through wash-and-set appointments, they called it "the Southern woman's Swiss Army knife." It could cut, comfort, condemn, or console—sometimes all at once.

"The trick," as Miss Mae would say while teasing another blue-haired crown, "is all in the delivery. It's like serving vinegar in a crystal glass—it's not what you say, it's how you sugar-coat it."

Sweet Southern Steel

Charles E. Cravey

Three words that dance on Southern air,

Wrapped in grace beyond compare.

Through sympathy or subtle slight,

These words can darken day or light.

Past meanings plain and meanings veiled,

Through social graces never failed,

The South's sweet sword cuts swift and sure.

In tones so kind, in words so pure.

For some speak plain what's on their mind,

While Southern folks keep things refined—

With phrases dipped in honey's art,

Like the simple "Well, bless your heart!"

Reflection on Southern Speech

In the South, we understand that language is an art form, that words can be wielded like fine surgical tools or wrapped like gifts in layers of meaning. "Bless your heart" teaches us that sometimes the kindest cut is the one wrapped in compassion, that truth doesn't always need to be naked to be true.

These words remind us that grace isn't just about being nice—it's about finding ways to navigate life's complexities with dignity intact, about keeping social fabric strong even when individual threads get snagged.

Because some phrases don't just speak—they perform a whole ballet of meaning in three simple words.

29

Two Birds – One Stone

A Southern Saying

Miss Maybell Jenkins always said efficiency was a Northern invention. Down here, we took our time with things, let them simmer proper-like. But one scorching Tuesday, when her prized tomatoes needed watering and her grandchild needed watching, she reckoned she'd try something new.

Little Tommy, barely knee-high to a grasshopper, stood watching his grandmother with curious eyes as she filled the old tin watering can. "Come here, sugar," she called, patting the red dirt beside her. "Want to help Mee-Maw water these tomatoes?"

Those little eyes lit up like lightning bugs on a June evening. For the next hour, Tommy learned about the delicate dance of nurturing plants while Miss Maybell learned something too - sometimes the best solution isn't about being efficient, it's about making moments matter double.

"You see," she told Tommy later, wiping sweat from her brow, "folks talk about killing two birds with one stone, but I reckon it's better to think about feeding two souls with one deed."

The Garden's Wisdom

Charles E. Cravey

In Grandma's garden, wisdom grows

Between the tomatoes, row by row

Where efficiency meets Southern grace,

And hurry has no welcome place.

Two birds, they say, one stone to throw,

But Grandma's way is soft and slow

For in the gentle art of time,

Two blessings bloom on one sweet vine.

The task at hand might double be,

But love makes work flow naturally.

Like morning glories climbing high,

Two purposes toward one blue sky.

Southern Philosophy

In the South, we understand that true efficiency isn't measured by the tasks we combine but by the connections we create. When we speak of "two birds, one stone," we're really talking about the art of mindful presence - how a single moment, properly tended, can nurture multiple blessings. Like a front porch that serves both as a gathering place and a cooling station on summer evenings, the richest experiences in life often serve more than one purpose. The wisdom lies not in the rushing, but in the recognition that some of life's sweetest moments come when we let purpose and pleasure intertwine, like morning glory vines on a garden fence.

30

Windcatcher

DOWN IN SAVANNAH, WHERE the Spanish moss drapes like nature's own lace curtains, old Mr. Thaddeus kept what folks called a windcatcher on his wraparound porch. Weren't nothing fancy - just a clever contraption of copper and tin that danced with every breeze. But Lord, the stories it could tell.

"You see," he'd say, rocking gently in his weathered chair, "them ancient folks in Persia knew something we done forgot. They built these tall towers that caught the wind like my mama used to catch fireflies in a jar - not to keep it, mind you, but to let it work its cooling magic."

Folks would gather on his porch during those sticky Georgia afternoons, watching his wind-catcher spin and swirl while the breeze it channeled made even August feel bearable. Some said it was just science, but Miss Eleanor from next door swore it was pure poetry - the way it turned hot air into sweet relief, like turning lemons into the coldest glass of summer lemonade.

"Nature provides," Mr. Thaddeus would remind us, his eyes twinkling like stars on a clear night. "We just got to be clever enough to catch what she's offering."

Whispers on the Wind

Charles E. Cravey

The windcatcher spins its tales today.

Like memories caught in summer's sway,

Dancing high above the ground,

Making music without a sound.

Ancient wisdom in modern air,

Cooling comfort beyond compare,

Persian dreams in Southern skies,

Where innovation never dies.

Like Spanish moss in a gentle breeze,

It shares its secrets with the trees.

Reminding us with every spin:

Sometimes old ways help us win.

Southern Philosophy

Here in the South, we've always known that wisdom doesn't always wear modern clothes. The windcatcher stands as testament to how sometimes the oldest solutions carry the deepest truths. Like our grandmother's remedies or our grandfather's weather predictions, these ancient technologies remind us that progress isn't always about moving forward - sometimes it's about remembering what we've left behind. In a world racing toward artificial cooling, the windcatcher whispers of a time when humans lived in harmony with nature's rhythms. It teaches us that true innovation might just be the art of rediscovering what our ancestors already knew: that the answers to our modern challenges might dance right above our heads, carried on the wings of the wind itself.

31

Brooklet Dreams

NINE MILES EAST OF Statesboro, where peanut fields stretch like quilts across red Georgia clay, sits Brooklet - a town that time seems to hug rather than pass by. Every September, when the air starts to soften and summer loosens its grip, the whole town comes alive with the Peanut Festival, a tradition that's been stitching generations together since 1990.

Miss Sarah Beth, who's lived here longer than most oak trees have stood, likes to sit on her porch at the corner of Parker and Lee streets, watching the town breathe. "Folks ask me why I never left," she says, smoothing her apron. "But they don't understand - in Brooklet, we don't just live in a place, we live in a story."

She's right about that. Here, where everybody knows everybody's mama and their mama's mama too, community isn't just a word - it's the morning gossip at the local diner, it's the Friday night lights at Southeast Bulloch, it's the way the whole town shows up when someone needs help, like streams flowing naturally to the same sweet river.

Small Town Symphony

Charles E. Cravey

In Brooklet's gentle morning light,

Where peanut blooms make fields turn bright,

Two thousand souls share one heart's song,

In harmony where they belong.

Through Parker Street and Church Road too,

Past shops where friendly faces grew,

The spirit of this Georgia place

Moves slow, with uncommon grace.

September brings the festival fair,

With tractor races, joy to share,

While Spanish moss and Southern pines

Watch over as the day declines.

Southern Philosophy

In the tapestry of Southern life, small towns like Brooklet serve as anchors in a world that spins faster every day. Here, where the population barely tops two thousand, we find a profound truth: community isn't measured by size but by the depth of connections. Like the peanut plants that thrive in our soil, we grow stronger through our roots - intertwined, interdependent, drawing strength from the same earth. The town's motto, "A Great Place to Live," isn't just civic pride talking; it's a philosophy about what matters most in life - not the pace of progress but the pause of belonging, not the rush of change but the rhythm of tradition. In Brooklet's quiet streets and friendly porches, we're reminded that sometimes the biggest truths come wrapped in the smallest packages, like wisdom passed down over sweet tea and porch swings.

32

Sweet Smoke Heaven

DOWN ON MAGNOLIA STREET, where the railroad tracks split the old part of town from the new, Miss Betty's smoke shack has been a beacon of slow-cooked wisdom since before color TV came to town. Started in her daddy's backyard with nothing but a rusty drum barrel and determination, this little slice of paradise tells a story deeper than its sauce and sweeter than its smoke.

"The secret," she'd say, mopping her brow with a flour-dusted apron, "ain't in no recipe - though my grandmama's special blend sure helps. It's in the waiting." Even now, after forty-some years of tending fires, she still believes good things come to those who watch the coals.

Inside that weathered building with its tin roof and screen door that slaps like a bass drum, time moves by the rhythm of smoking meat and sharing stories. The walls, decorated with faded photographs and yesterday's memories, hold four decades of community like smoke holds flavor. Here, every rib that falls off the bone carries a piece of history, every bite of brisket tells a tale of patience, and every plate serves up a slice of heaven wrapped in Southern tradition.

Sweet Smoke Rising

Charles E. Cravey

Through decades deep as pit smoke blue,

Where patience makes old flavors new,

The stories rise like summer heat,

Where sauce and soul and service meet.

In heaven's kitchen, time runs slow,

While tender meats turn perfect so,

And wisdom seasons every bite,

Till everything comes out just right.

Four decades, flames still bright,

Making days turn tender night,

In this place where angels dare

To taste what love and time prepare.

Southern Philosophy

Down here, we understand that barbecue isn't just cooking - it's a meditation on time and transformation. Like the old-timers prove, true mastery isn't found in rushing but in the willingness to wait, to watch, to tend. A smoke shack is more than just a restaurant; it's a sanctuary where patience becomes flavor and tradition becomes taste. In a world obsessed with instant everything, these sacred spaces remind us that some flavors can only be coaxed out slowly, some wisdom can only be earned through years, and some heavens are built right here on earth, one patient hour at a time. It's not just about the meat - it's about the meeting of time, tradition, and tender care that transforms the ordinary into the divine.

33

Bainbridge, Georgia

OLD MISS MARTHA MAE Henderson could tell you everything about Bainbridge from her wraparound porch on Broad Street. "Sit yourself down," she'd say, pouring sweet tea into glasses that once belonged to her grandmother. "Let me tell you about this river town."

Where the Flint River meets Lake Seminole, Miss Martha Mae has watched Bainbridge stand like a testament to Southern grace for all her eighty-three years. Her daddy was harbormaster back when the port still buzzed with cotton barges, and she remembers every story, every change, every season of this town's becoming.

"People ask me why the bass grow so big here," she says, rocking slowly in her mother's old chair. "I tell 'em it's because the fish have been listening to Bainbridge stories for so long, they just can't help but grow wise and strong themselves." Her laugh ripples like the river water, deep and knowing.

From her porch, Willis Park spreads out like a green jewel in the city's crown, its gazebo still proud as a Sunday hat. She points out the old brick buildings that line the square, telling tales of each one - which ones hosted their first kisses, which ones survived the big storm of '42, which ones still hold secrets in their shadows.

River City Rhythms

Charles E. Cravey

Miss Martha's memories flow like wine,

Through years of change and grand design,

Where Flint meets Seminole's wide shore,

And stories drift from every door.

Through Willis Park the seasons turn,

While ancient oaks stand proud and stern,

Their branches heavy with the weight

Of tales they're longing to relate.

Deep roots reach down through red clay soil,

While progress blooms from ancient toil,

In this place where waters meet,

And Southern hearts still keep their beat.

Southern Philosophy

Miss Martha Mae knows what most folks take years to learn - that a town isn't just streets and buildings but a living tapestry of stories woven together by time and memory. In Bainbridge, where the rivers meet, we understand that progress doesn't mean forgetting; it means building bridges between what was and what could be. Like the waters that shaped our shores, life here flows with its own particular wisdom. We're more than just the Bass Capital of Georgia -we're keepers of a tradition that says community isn't just where you live, it's how you live. Here, where porch swings still keep time with Southern summers and downtown strolls remain an evening ritual, we've learned that tomorrow tastes sweetest when seasoned with yesterday's memories.

34

Ludowici

MISS PEARL WILSON SAT in her white wooden rocker on the corner of Main Street, right where she could see both the courthouse and the old Well Pavilion. At ninety-two, she'd seen more changes than most oak trees, and like those oaks, she'd grown deep roots in this small Georgia town.

"Back when I was just a slip of a girl," she'd tell anyone who'd listen, "this town was known for them fancy roof tiles. The Dixie plant covered more ground than a country mile". Her eyes would drift to the courthouse's clay-tiled roof, one of the few remaining crowns of Ludowici's golden age.

These days, the town moved slower than Sunday afternoon, which suited Miss Pearl just fine. She remembered when Highway 301 brought a steady stream of Florida-bound tourists through town, back before Interstate 95 drew them away like a river changing course. "Some folks called us a speed trap," she'd chuckle, smoothing her floral dress. "But honey, we were just trying to get them Yankees to slow down long enough to taste our hospitality."

The Well Pavilion stood across the way, its weathered frame a testament to simpler times when townsfolk gathered for cool water and warmer conversation. "That well," Miss Pearl would say, "gave more than water. It gave us community."

Long County's Heart

Charles E. Cravey

Where highway meets the old dirt road,

Where stories sleep and dreams unfold,

A town that time seems to embrace,

Keeps Southern charm and gentle grace.

The courthouse stands in brick and pride.

While memories flow like morning tide,

Of tile-topped roofs and tourist days,

When life moved slow through summer haze.

The well still whispers tales of old,

Of secrets sweet and stories told,

In this small town where time runs deep,

And Georgia's heart finds peace to keep.

Southern Philosophy

Here in Ludowici, we understand that a town's worth isn't measured by its size but by the depth of its stories. Like the clay that once shaped our famous tiles, we've been molded by time and tradition into something uniquely Southern. Some might see just another small Georgia town, but we know better -we're a living reminder that the best things in life can't be rushed, that community isn't built overnight, and that true wealth isn't in speed but in the willingness to slow down and savor what matters. The Well Pavilion still stands as our philosopher's stone, teaching us that the sweetest waters are drawn from the deepest wells of memory and connection.

35

Coastal Rhythms

KING'S BAY, GEORGIA

WHERE THE MARSHLANDS KISS the Atlantic, nestled between live oaks draped in Spanish moss, King's Bay holds its secrets like an oyster holds its pearl. Miss Virginia Lee Tidewater has lived here since before the Navy came, back when this was just a sleepy coastal town where shrimpers cast their nets into the misty dawn.

"Lord have mercy," she says from her screened porch overlooking the salt marsh, "you should've seen this place before all of them submarines showed up." Her eyes, bright as marsh water at sunrise, sparkle with memories. "Course, we're proud of our sailors now -they're family too."

At eighty-seven, Miss Virginia Lee remembers when the loudest sound was mullet jumping in the creek, before the deep thrumming of nuclear subs became the town's heartbeat. She tends her garden of camellias and azaleas, just like her mama did, while across the marsh, modern warriors train in ancient waters.

"Some folks say we lost something when the base came," she muses, stirring her sweet tea with a sprig of mint, "but I reckon we just added new chapters to an old story. Like when the tide comes in - it doesn't wash away the marsh, it just makes it deeper."

Coastal Rhythms

Charles E. Cravey

Where submarine meets shrimp boat wake,

Where past and present gently shake

Hands across the brackish tide,

Old South and New walk side by side.

Through live oak halls and Spanish lace,

Time moves with military grace.

While marsh hens call their ancient song

To sailors who now march along.

Deep waters hide their secrets well.

While surface stories sweetly tell

Of times when simple fishers knew

These waters that now serve the Blue.

Southern Philosophy

Here in King's Bay, we've learned that change doesn't have to mean surrender - it can mean growth, like a salt marsh adapting to the tides. Our town stands as a testament to how tradition and progress can dance together, like dolphins playing in a submarine's wake. We understand that strength comes in many forms: in the quiet power of a nuclear submarine, in the patient persistence of a shrimper mending nets, and in the resilient spirit of a community that knows how to bend without breaking. Like our marshlands, we absorb what comes, filter what matters, and emerge richer for the mixture of salt and fresh, old, and new, civilian and military, all flowing together in one deep, complex tide of Southern life.

36

Cordele, Georgia

A SOUTHERN TALE

Miss Evelyn Grace Tucker sat in her favorite chair at the Cordele Dispatch office, where she'd worked as a reporter since 1962. At eighty-two, she'd written more stories about the "Watermelon Capital of the World" than there were seeds in a Sugar Baby melon, and she wasn't done yet.

"Used to be," she'd say, adjusting her cat-eyeglasses, "you couldn't drive down any street in July without seeing pickup trucks loaded with watermelons, headed to the Farmer's Market. The whole town smelled sweet enough to make the angels jealous." Her fingers, still nimble from decades of typing, would tap rhythmically on her desk as she spoke.

From her second-floor window, she could see the old railroad tracks where the SAM Shortline still chugged along, carrying tourists instead of produce now. That iron crossing of rails had birthed Cordele back in 1888, and Miss Evelyn swore you could still hear the whispers of history in every train whistle.

"We've got that big rocket out on I-75," she'd tell visitors, "But our real claim to fame is sweeter than any metal monument. It's in the juice running down your arm from a fresh-picked melon, in the 'yes ma'ams' and 'no sirs' still taught to children, in the way folks wave whether they know you or not."

Watermelon Dreams

Charles E. Cravey

Where rail lines cross like silver threads,

Through melon fields and watershed,

A town grows sweet with summer's gift,

While history makes the present shift.

Through market stalls and depot days,

Past rocket tall and sun-bright ways,

The stories flow like melon wine.

Along each weathered railroad line.

In summer's heat the truth grows clear,

Why heaven dropped its sweetness here,

Where watermelon hearts beat strong,

And trains still sing their iron song.

Southern Philosophy

Here in Cordele, we understand that sweetness isn't just about taste - it's about the way life ripens in its own perfect time. Like a watermelon thumped just right, our town resonates with a depth that only patience can produce. We're more than just a stop between Macon and Florida; we're a place where the rhythms of agriculture still dance with the pulse of progress, where trains still matter, and where the simple pleasure of a cold slice of melon on a hot day remains one of life's profound truths. Some might see just another small Georgia town, but we know that, like the best watermelons, true beauty lies beneath the surface, in the heart where sweetness grows.

37

Sandy Springs

A Southern Tale

Miss Catherine Abernathy remembered when Sandy Springs was nothing but wooded hills and bubbling springs, before the glass towers stretched toward heaven and the traffic hummed like angry bees. From her family's old homestead - now surrounded by progress but still standing proud - she'd watch the city grow like kudzu after a summer rain.

"Folks ask me if I miss the old days," she'd say, tending her prized tea roses that her grandmother had planted. "But honey, this place has always been about moving forward while keeping your roots deep." At seventy-eight, she'd seen Sandy Springs transform from quiet countryside to Atlanta's ambitious sister yet somehow maintain its own distinct personality.

From her garden, she could see the modern skyline of Pill Hill rising above the trees, where doctors now practiced their healing arts not far from where her great-grandmother once gathered herbs for remedies. The natural spring that gave the city its name still flowed nearby, though most folks hurrying past didn't know it was there.

"We may have fancy restaurants and high-rise living now," she'd tell visitors, her blue eyes twinkling, "but underneath all that shine, we're still a community built around springs and Southern values. Some things even progress can't wash away."

City in the Trees

Charles E. Cravey

Where ancient springs still softly flow,

Beneath glass towers' modern glow,

A city rises, proud and new,

While holding old truths tried and true.

Through Roswell Road's eternal stream,

Past Mercedes' silver gleam,

The spirit of this place remains.

Like sunshine after summer rains.

Though progress marches day by day,

Some things time cannot sweep away:

The springs that gave this place its start

Still bubble in the city's heart.

Southern Philosophy

Here in Sandy Springs, we've learned that progress doesn't have to mean forgetting. Like the natural springs that still flow beneath our modern streets, the old ways nourish the new. We understand that true growth isn't just about building higher - it's about digging deeper, keeping those connections to what matters most. Some see us as just another suburb, but we know better. We're a place where Southern hospitality meets modern opportunity, where ancient springs and glass towers coexist in perfect harmony, and where community isn't just a word but a way of life that flows as steady as the waters that gave us our name. In Sandy Springs, we've mastered the art of embracing tomorrow while keeping yesterday close to our hearts.

38

Fighting With Monsters

OLD JUDGE MASON SAT on his back porch in the Georgia twilight, watching fireflies rise from his wife's garden like scattered stars. After forty years on the bench, he'd seen enough of humanity's darkness to know that monsters weren't just things that lived under children's beds.

"The trouble with fighting monsters," he'd tell his grandson Tommy, who'd recently joined the public defender's office, "is keeping your own heart from turning hard as Georgia clay in August." His weathered hands would smooth over the arm of his rocking chair, worn smooth by years of contemplation.

Tommy had come seeking wisdom after a particularly difficult case. The judge's eyes, soft with understanding beneath his silver brows, held decades of similar struggles. "When I first started," he continued, "I thought everything was black and white, good and evil. But Lord, if life doesn't teach you about them shades of gray."

From his porch, the garden his wife had planted forty years ago still bloomed - roses alongside thorns, beauty persisting despite the darkness. "The real victory," he'd say, watching a cardinal settle into the crepe myrtle for the night, "isn't in defeating the monsters. It's in remembering your own humanity while facing them."

Twilight Wisdom

Charles E. Cravey

When darkness creeps through evening shade,

And monsters from our nightmares fade

Into the faces that we know,

The lines between friend, foe, run low.

Through courthouse halls and garden ways,

Past judgment's swift and certain days,

The truth grows clear as morning light:

Not all that's dark lacks threads of bright.

In battles fought with soul and mind,

The hardest victory's to find

The grace to stand both firm and true,

While keeping mercy's heart in view.

Southern Philosophy

Down here in the South, we understand that the greatest battles aren't fought with fists or firearms, but within the human heart. Like kudzu covering both mansion and shack alike, darkness doesn't discriminate - but neither does light. We've learned that justice without mercy is like a summer without rain, and that the true measure of character isn't in how hard you can fight, but in how well you can hold onto your humanity while facing life's darkest corners. Some say you can't fight monsters without becoming one, but we know better. The secret lies in remembering that even the darkest night holds stars, and that sometimes the bravest thing isn't in winning the fight, but in keeping your soul intact through it all.

39

Nothing Lasts Forever!

MISS ADELAIDE BEAUMONT STOOD in her kitchen, surrounded by the last of her grandmother's china - most of it wrapped in newspaper, ready for packing. The old family home on Peachtree had been sold, its grand rooms soon to be replaced by something modern and sleek.

"Sugar," she said to her granddaughter helping her pack, "some folks think holding on tight makes things last forever." Her hands, elegant despite their age, traced the gold rim of her grandmother's teacup. "But that's about as useful as trying to catch morning mist in a mason jar."

At seventy-five, Miss Adelaide had watched Atlanta transform from a genteel Southern city to a bustling metropolis. She'd seen forests become shopping centers, dirt roads turn to highways, and old friends fade away like morning glories at dusk. Yet her smile remained as bright as Georgia sunshine.

"The secret," she'd say, carefully wrapping the teacup in paper, "isn't in keeping things from changing. It's in learning to dance with the change itself. Like my mama used to say - everything's temporary, even the things marked 'permanent.'"

Time's Sweet Flow

Charles E. Cravey

Like Spanish moss in autumn breeze,

Like shadows cast by ancient trees,

All precious things must have their day,

Then softly, sweetly slip away.

Through rooms where memories still dance,

Past moments caught in time's romance,

The truth flows clear as summer wine:

Nothing stays forever fine.

But in the letting go, we find

The sweetest gifts are left behind:

Not in the things we try to hold,

But in the stories left untold.

Southern Philosophy

Here in the South, we understand that impermanence isn't a curse but a blessing in disguise. Like the changing seasons that paint our magnolias first in white blooms and then in green strength, life moves in cycles of letting go and beginning anew. We've learned that trying to freeze time is like trying to catch lightning in a bottle - beautiful in theory but impossible in practice. The true art lies not in preserving everything forever, but in appreciating the beauty of each passing moment, each fading sunset, each changing season. Some say nothing gold can stay, and they're right - but it's that very transience that makes the gold shine brighter, the memories sweeter, and the present moment more precious. In the end, what lasts isn't the china or the silver or even the grand old homes - it's the love we share, the stories we tell, and the grace with which we learn to let go.

40

Don't Take Tomorrow for Granted

MISS ELEANOR JAMES WOKE every morning at five-thirty to watch the sun rise over her peach orchard, a ritual she'd kept since her husband passed ten years ago. This morning, as steam rose from her coffee cup like morning fog off the pond, she noticed her youngest grandson, Tyler, sitting on the porch steps, troubled by life's uncertainties.

"You know," she said, settling into her worn wicker chair, "your grandaddy used to say worrying about tomorrow is like trying to eat next week's cornbread today." Her soft laugh drifted across the morning air like chimney smoke. "Can't be done, and it just spoils your appetite for what's right in front of you."

At eighty-four, Miss Eleanor had buried a husband, survived two hurricanes, and seen more sunrises than she could count. Each morning's light painted the peach trees in colors that would never quite be repeated, teaching her daily that every moment was its own kind of miracle.

"The trick isn't in planning for tomorrow," she told Tyler, watching the sun gild the orchards in morning gold. "It's in living today so full and sweet that tomorrow has something worth building on."

Dawn's Promise

Charles E. Cravey

Each sunrise brings a gift untold,

Each moment spins its thread of gold,

Through peach-bloom days and starlit nights,

Through simple joys and sacred sites.

Tomorrow's not a promised thing.

Like mockingbirds that might not sing,

But today spreads wide and true,

A feast of hours, fresh as dew.

So, gather sweet while morning gleams,

And plant today with hopeful dreams,

For wisdom whispers soft and low:

Now's the only time we know.

Southern Philosophy

Down here in Georgia's gentle heart, we understand that tomorrow is like a morning glory - beautiful to imagine but never guaranteed to bloom. We've learned through generations of sunrises and sunsets that life's sweetest moments don't come with warranties or promises. They come in the simple grace of now - in the taste of fresh peaches, in the song of whippoorwills, in the laughter of loved ones gathered close. Some folks spend so much time reaching for tomorrow that they miss the miracle happening right under their feet. But we know better. Like morning dew on spiderwebs, each moment sparkles with its own brief, beautiful light. The true art of living isn't in banking on tomorrow's dreams but in weaving today's moments into something so beautiful that tomorrow, should it come, has a solid foundation to build upon.

41

Walking in High Cotton

Miss Augusta Weatherby stood in her family's cotton field, running her fingers across the soft white bolls that stretched toward the horizon like summer clouds brought down to earth. At eighty-nine, she'd seen more cotton seasons than most folks had seen Christmas mornings.

"People nowadays," she'd tell her great-granddaughter Sarah, "hear 'walking in high cotton' and think it's just about being prosperous. But child, it's about something deeper than money." Her eyes, bright as morning dew, scanned the rows her family had tended for generations.

The cotton stood chest-high this year - a blessing that would've made her daddy smile. "When cotton grows tall and full," she explained, "picking it means you can stand up straight while you work. No breaking your back bending down. That's what walking in high cotton really means - dignity in your labor, pride in your harvest, and hope rising tall as these plants."

From her back porch, where the old rocking chair kept time with memory, the white fields glowed in the afternoon sun like promises kept. "Life ain't always about being rich," she'd say, "but about standing tall through whatever season you're given."

Cotton Wisdom

Charles E. Cravey

Through fields of white in autumn light,

Where hopes grow tall and dreams take flight,

The cotton stands like morning prayer.

While wisdom floats on evening air.

Each boll holds more than fiber's gift.

More than market prices lift,

They carry stories, soft and true,

Of standing tall in morning dew.

In rows that stretch toward heaven's gate,

Where pride and promise congregate,

We learn to walk with heads held high.

Between the cotton and the sky.

Southern Philosophy

Here in the South, we understand that true wealth isn't just about what's in your wallet - it's about what's in your heart. Like cotton growing tall in fertile soil, prosperity has deep roots in dignity, hard work, and hope. We've learned through generations that walking in high cotton isn't just about having plenty - it's about carrying yourself with grace through both abundance and scarcity. Some might see just another crop in these white fields, but we know better. Each row tells a story of persistence, each boll holds a lesson about patience, and every harvest reminds us that the sweetest rewards come from keeping faith through all seasons. In the end, walking in high cotton is as much about the journey as the destination - it's about holding your head high no matter how tall or short your cotton grows.

42

Madder Than a Wet Hen!

MISS HATTIE MAE WILKERSON'S temper was legendary in three counties, but her heart was pure gold. From her wraparound porch in South Georgia, she'd dispense both wisdom and warnings with equal measure, her silver hair caught up in a bun tight as her principles.

"Land sakes," she'd declare, fanning herself with yesterday's church bulletin, "folks these days don't know what real mad is. Back when I was coming up, Mama would say 'madder than a wet hen' and everybody knew exactly what that meant." Her blue eyes would spark like summer lightning at the memory.

Young folks would gather on her porch steps to hear how the saying came about. "See here," she'd explain, smoothing her apron, "when a hen gets too broody, won't leave her nest even when there ain't no eggs to hatch, farmers would dunk her in cold water. And Lord have mercy, ain't nothing in this world madder than a soaking wet hen with ruffled dignity!"

At eighty-six, Miss Hattie Mae had learned to temper her own quick temper with wisdom earned through years. "Sometimes," she'd say with a knowing smile, "getting your feathers ruffled is just life's way of teaching you to shake it off and start fresh."

Ruffled Feathers

Charles E. Cravey

When anger rises hot as June,

Like thunder rolling much too soon,

Remember what the wet hens know:

Some flames just need a chance to glow.

Through feathers ruffled, pride awry,

Past moments when we'd rather fly,

The wisdom comes in nature's way:

Tomorrow's always fresh as May.

So let your temper have its dance,

Then give your spirit second chance.

For wisdom whispers soft and clear:

Peace returns when skies grow clear.

Southern Philosophy

Down here in the South, we understand that anger, like summer storms, has its place in nature's order. Just as a wet hen eventually dries her feathers and returns to scratch contentedly in the yard, we learn that temporary upset doesn't define us - it refines us. Some folks think showing anger isn't proper, but we know better. Like those old hens, sometimes you need to get your feathers ruffled to appreciate the comfort of smooth ones. The real wisdom isn't in never getting mad - it's in knowing how to shake off the water, smooth down your feathers, and get back to the business of living. After all, even the hottest Georgia day ends with a cool evening breeze.

43

Pretty as a Peach

MISS ANNABELLE MERIWETHER SAT at her vanity, gently patting rose-water on her cheeks just like her mama taught her seventy years ago. Outside her window, the peach orchard her grandfather planted stretched out like a pastel painting in the morning light.

"Beauty's got layers," she'd tell her granddaughter Emma, who was always rushing through her morning routine. "Just like a perfect peach - there's the blush on the skin, the sweetness inside, and right at the heart, there's something strong enough to grow a whole new tree."

At eighty-two, Miss Annabelle's face had collected its share of laugh lines and memories, each one earned through years of Georgia summers. Her silver hair caught the morning light like Spanish moss in moonshine, and her eyes still sparkled with the same mischief that had captured her late husband's heart in 1955.

"When folks say, 'pretty as a peach,'" she'd explain, dabbing perfume behind her ears, "they ain't just talking about what meets the eye. They're talking about something that ripens slow and sweet, that takes sun and rain and time to reach its perfect moment."

Peach Blossom Wisdom

Charles E. Cravey

Through orchard rows where beauty grows,

Past morning light where time slows,

The peach trees teach their gentle art:

True grace blooms from the heart.

Like velvet skin in summer's glow,

Some things take time to grow and show.

Their sweetness earned through rain and shine,

Till beauty proves itself divine.

So wear your years like nature's lace,

Let wisdom paint your glowing face.

For beauty's truth grows ever clear:

It ripens sweeter year by year.

Southern Philosophy

Here in Georgia, we understand that true beauty has more to do with ripening than with remaining young. Like our famous peaches, the sweetest qualities take time to develop - a blush earned from sunshine, character shaped by storms, and wisdom that grows deeper with each passing season. Some folks think beauty is only skin deep, but we know better. Real beauty, like a perfect peach, requires patience. It needs both sunshine and rain, both warm days and cool nights, both tender care and the courage to weather whatever comes. In the end, being "pretty as a peach" isn't about perfection - it's about developing that rare combination of outer grace and inner sweetness that, like the best Georgia peaches, only gets better with time.

44

Nahunta

AN INTRIGUING SOUTHERN TOWN

MISS RUBY MAE COLLINS sat in her favorite porch rocker, watching the evening trains rumble through downtown Nahunta. At eighty-seven, she'd seen this railroad town transform from a bustling turpentine hub to a quiet crossroads where highways 301 and 82 stretched out like lazy arms toward distant places.

"You know," she'd tell her great-grandson Tommy, "folks used to call this place 'tall trees' in the Indian tongue. Back then, the pines stretched up so high they seemed to scratch the very face of heaven." Her eyes, bright as morning dew on wiregrass, would drift to where those ancient forests once stood.

The trains still came, though not as many as before. Each whistle brought memories of when Nahunta was the heart of Brantley County's timber empire, when the air smelled of pine sap and possibility. "We even had us an armadillo festival once," she'd chuckle, smoothing her apron. "Brought more folks to town than we had chairs to seat 'em in."

"Some say nothing much happens in Nahunta anymore," she'd muse, watching the evening sun paint the sky in colors that would've made any artist weep. "But honey, they just don't know how to listen to the quiet stories this town still tells."

Crossroads Dreams

Charles E. Cravey

Where highways cross and trains still sing,

Past memories that softly cling

To corners where tall trees once grew,

And history drips like morning dew.

Through quiet streets and gentle days,

Where time moves slow in Southern ways,

The spirit of this special place

Keeps flowing with unhurried grace.

Though forests fell and times have changed,

Some precious things remain unchanged:

The warmth of hearts, the friendly ways,

The peace of slow-lived Southern days.

Southern Philosophy

Here in Nahunta, we understand that significance isn't measured by size but by the depth of roots sunk into Georgia soil. Like the tall trees that gave us our name, we stand firmly planted in who we are, reaching skyward while keeping our foundation strong. Some folks might see just another small town where highways meet, but we know better. Every train whistle carries echoes of our past, every friendly wave holds the promise of our future, and every sunset reminds us that beauty doesn't need an audience to be profound. In Nahunta, we've learned that the richest stories often come wrapped in the quietest moments, and that sometimes the greatest wisdom grows in the smallest places.

45

Grand Old Victorian

WHERE TIME TAKES TEA

THERE SHE STANDS ON Savannah Street, her lace-like gingerbread eaves dripping with the melody of frozen music, as proud as any Southern belle who has weathered a century's storms. The Morrison House—that's the name still whispered among the townsfolk, though the Morrisons departed during the era of Truman.

Three stories of painted lady splendor rise majestically, with a wrap-around porch spacious enough for Sunday afternoon musings and a witness to more marriage proposals than the town's own church. Her stained-glass transom captures the morning light with a divine touch, casting rainbow blessings upon heart pine floors that have creaked under the weight of five generations.

Miss Adelaide Jenkins, the devoted caretaker of this venerable beauty, knows every secret whispered within those walls. "A house like this," she muses, gently adjusting the lace curtains in the parlor, "isn't merely a structure—it's a keeper of memories. Each squeaky floorboard tells a tale, every scratched doorframe marks a child's ascent, and each worn stair step counts a thousand comings and goings."

Though the town has transformed around her, the grand old Victorian stands resolute, her turret overseeing a world in flux while her rooms cradle the grace of yesteryears.

The Lady's Watch

Charles E. Cravey

Where gingerbread meets morning light,

And memories dance in shadows bright,

The painted lady holds her ground.

While modern chaos swirls around.

Through crystal panes and wooden lace,

Past years of change she shows her grace.

Each room still holds its stories dear.

In walls that whisper, "History's here."

For some homes simply shelter give.

While others teach us how to live—

In grace notes carved in yesteryear,

Still singing sweet for those who hear.

Reflection on Living History

In the South, we understand that some houses are more than shelter—they're anchors that hold communities to their past, lighthouses that guide us toward grace. These grand old Victorians remind us that beauty isn't just about perfection—it's about perseverance, about maintaining dignity even as paint peels and porch boards sag.

These homes teach us that true elegance never goes out of style, that some things are worth preserving, and that the best way to honor the past is to keep it alive in the present.

Because some houses don't just stand—they stand for something. They become symbols of resilience, embodying the spirit of those who came before us. The stories embedded within their walls are not merely echoes of the past but vibrant reminders that each creak and groan is part of a living tapestry, weaving together the fabric of a shared heritage.

In their halls, laughter from bygone eras still lingers, and the scent of old wood mingles with memories of family gatherings, celebrations, and quiet moments of reflection. These houses, like the Morrison House, are repositories of dreams and aspirations, of lives lived with purpose and passion.

As we walk their storied halls, we become part of their narrative, adding our own chapters to the ever-evolving tale. We learn to appreciate the beauty in imperfection, to find strength in continuity, and to cherish the fleeting moments of grace that these grand dames of architecture offer to those who pause to listen.

In preserving them, we preserve a piece of ourselves, ensuring that the lessons they impart continue to guide future generations. Let us hold them dear, for in their steadfast presence, they remind us not only of where we come from but of who we are and who we might yet become.

46

Mitigating Circumstances

A TALE OF SOUTHERN JUSTICE

JUDGE EMMA MAE BLACKWOOD had sat on the bench in the Meriwether County courthouse long enough to know that truth, like kudzu, often grew in unexpected directions. Today's case seemed simple enough: Bobby Ray Jenkins had stolen Mrs. Patterson's prize-winning tomatoes right off her vine. But in small Southern towns, nothing's ever quite that straightforward.

"Your Honor," Bobby Ray stood, his weathered hands gripping his cap, "I admit to taking them tomatoes. But see, my mama's been laid up sick, and all she talked about was wanting one more taste of summer, like Mrs. Patterson's daddy used to grow when they was kids together."

Mrs. Patterson, who'd come to court ready for righteous indignation, sat a little straighter in her witness chair. The mention of her daddy, known county-wide for his Cherokee Purple tomatoes, softened something in her face.

"The circumstances," Judge Emma Mae would later write in her journal, "often carry more truth than the crime itself." She paused, looking over her spectacles at Bobby Ray. His eyes were earnest, and there was a flicker of desperation mingled with hope. The courtroom was silent, the air heavy with the weight of shared history and unspoken understanding.

Judge Emma Mae leaned forward slightly, her voice gentle but firm. "Mr. Jenkins, while the law does not condone theft, it does recognize the complexities of human need. Mrs. Patterson, would you be open to discussing a way for Mr. Jenkins to make amends without further legal action?"

Mrs. Patterson hesitated, glancing around at her neighbors who filled the benches behind her. The room was full of nods and murmurs of agreement—this was a community that valued reconciliation over retribution.

"Well, Your Honor," she began, her voice softening further, "I reckon Bobby Ray could help tend to my garden for the rest of the season. Those vines can be a bit unruly, and I could use the help."

Bobby Ray's face broke into a relieved smile, and he nodded vigorously. "Yes, ma'am. I'd be more than happy to do that."

Judge Emma Mae nodded, a small smile playing at the corners of her lips. "Then let it be so. Let your actions cultivate not just tomatoes, but also goodwill and understanding."

As the gavel came down, sealing the unusual resolution, the courtroom exhaled collectively, the tension easing into a shared sense of community restored. For in Meriwether County, justice was not just about the letter of the law but the spirit of compassion and neighborly love.

Justice's Garden

Charles E. Cravey

Where truth grows wild like summer vines,

Past simple laws and straight-drawn lines,

The heart of justice often leads

Through tangled tales and human needs.

Some wrongs need more than judgment's weight—

They need the grace to contemplate.

The deeper roots of why we fall,

And mercy's wisdom through it all.

For some see black and others white,

While wisdom seeks the softer light —

Where understanding's gentle art

Can heal what tore two souls apart.

Reflection on Southern Justice

In the South, we embrace the notion that justice transcends mere punishment—often, it dances in the realm of restoration, seeking to weave together the frayed threads of our community. We recognize that, like summer storms, life's tempests can compel even the noblest souls to act in desperation.

These moments within the courthouse illuminate the truth that genuine justice bears a human visage; at times, the most profound verdict resides not in legal tomes but within empathetic hearts. They serve as poignant reminders that each case unfolds its own narrative, as distinct as a finger-print and often as intricate as the tapestry of family heritage.

For there are circumstances that do not merely soften the edges of judgment—they shine a light on the very essence of justice itself.

47

Endless Rows of Corn

A Southern Symphony in Green

From the winding back roads of Mitchell County, the cornfields rise toward the heavens like verdant cathedral walls. Row upon perfect row stretches onward, marching to the distant horizon where earth and sky kiss in a shimmering embrace of Georgia heat. For city dwellers, it may appear monotonous—the same vista echoed a thousand times. Yet, seasoned farmers like Jesse Macintyre perceive a deeper truth.

"Every row tells its own tale," Jesse muses, his weathered fingers gliding over silk-topped stalks. "This row here recalls the spring drought, while that one over yonder holds the memory of May's full moon. Some rows whisper, some sing, but they all possess something to convey if you know how to listen."

His grandson Tyler, back from Georgia Tech for summer respite, traverses these rows as if reading braille—sensing the subtle variances in each stalk's posture, observing how morning dew beads differently where red clay meets loam. He's discovering what his grandfather has always understood: that farming transcends mere planting of seeds in straight lines—it's about deciphering the epic poem inscribed in soil and sun.

As the evening light cascades golden through the stalks, it transforms each row into a corridor of stained glass, with every leaf a panel narrating its own saga of survival, growth, and grace.

Cornrow Chronicles

Charles E. Cravey

Where endless green meets endless sky,

And summer breezes softly sigh,

Each perfect row its tale unfolds,

In stories, only farmers hold.

Through morning mist and midday heat,

Past where the earth and heaven meet,

These living walls their wisdom share,

In whispers carried on the air.

For some see sameness, stretching far,

While others read each leafy scar—

The testament of sun and rain,

Written in rows of golden grain.

Reflection on Growing Wisdom

In the South, we understand that monotony is just mystery waiting to be revealed. These cornrows teach us that patience isn't just about waiting—it's about watching, listening, and learning the subtle languages of growth and change.

These fields remind us that life's greatest lessons often come disguised as repetition, that wisdom grows best in straight lines tended with loving care, and that every harvest starts with faith planted in furrows.

Because some rows don't just grow corn—they grow understanding. And as the seasons turn, the lessons deepen. Each rustle of leaves in the wind is a gentle reminder that life, much like these fields, is a tapestry woven with moments of perseverance and grace. The sun's rise and fall mark time, but within that rhythmic cycle, there's a quiet revolution of transformation, of seeds becoming sustenance.

In the evening, when the fireflies dance among the corn, their delicate glow mirrors the sparks of insight that come to those patient enough to pause and ponder. It's in these tranquil moments that we find clarity, realizing that the simple act of nurturing a crop is akin to nurturing the soul.

So, when the harvest finally arrives, it's not just the bounty of corn we celebrate. We honor the journey, the stories told through each rusted husk, and the wisdom gleaned from the steadfast soil. In these rows, we see the reflection of our own lives—where every challenge faced and every victory earned becomes part of a greater narrative of growth and resilience.

48

"Johnny-on-the-Spot"

A Southern Second Chance

Down at Miller's Hardware in downtown Bainbridge, everybody knew if you needed something done right and done quick, you called Johnny Tate. Didn't matter if it was a leaky roof at midnight or a stuck tractor at dawn—Johnny would show up, tools in hand, wearing that same faded Braves cap he'd had since the '95 Series.

Folks didn't talk much about where Johnny came from or about those dark years he spent up at Reidsville State Prison. What mattered was who he'd become: the man who never said no, never showed up late, and never left a job half-done.

"Lord gives us all second chances," Johnny would say, adjusting that weathered cap. "Some folks just recognize them better than others." His chance had come in the form of old Mr. Miller, who believed that a man's future mattered more than his past.

Now, twenty years later, Johnny's phone still rang day and night. "Johnny on the spot," he'd answer every single time, like those words were a promise, a prayer, and a redemption song all rolled into one.

The Spot Where Grace Lives

Charles E. Cravey

Where second chances bloom like spring,

And redemption spreads its healing wing,

Some souls find strength to rise again,

Through work and faith and helping then.

Past shadows dark of yesterday,

Through dawn that brings a brighter way,

The man who shows up, rain or shine,

Finds grace in being right on time.

For some see just a handyman.

While others glimpse redemption's plan—

How helping hands and faithful hearts

Give broken lives their second starts.

Reflection on Timely Grace

In the South, we understand that reliability isn't just about being on time—it's about being there when it matters, about proving your worth one fixed problem at a time. We know that reputation isn't inherited—it's built nail by nail, call by call, dawn by dawn.

These stories remind us that everyone deserves a chance to rewrite their story, that sometimes the measure of a man isn't where he started but how far he's willing to go to make things right.

Because some spots aren't just places—they're opportunities to prove grace works in real time.

And so, in the heart of Bainbridge, with its red-brick roads and dogwood-lined streets, Johnny Tate stood as a testament to the power of perseverance and the magic of second chances. His story was woven into the fabric of the community, a reminder that redemption is not just a distant dream but a living, breathing reality.

Neighbors would often see him at the diner, sharing a cup of coffee with Mr. Miller, or volunteering at the local church, hammer in hand, ready to lend his skills to whatever needed fixing. Every interaction, every smile exchanged, was a stitch in the tapestry of trust he had carefully crafted over the years.

Children who once watched him from a distance now ran to greet him, eager to hear tales of how he made the impossible possible. They learned from Johnny that even the toughest problems could be tackled with patience and heart and that true strength lay in the willingness to try again, no matter the odds.

In the quiet moments, when the work was done and the town lay still under a blanket of stars, Johnny would look out at the horizon and tip his

Braves cap to the heavens. He knew that while a man's hands could mend broken things, it was the grace of the second chance that truly repaired the soul.

And so, the legend of Johnny on the Spot continued to grow, whispered in hushed tones, and celebrated in stories shared across kitchen tables and front porches. A living lesson that in the South, and perhaps everywhere, the greatest gift we can give one another is the belief in what can be possible when we are willing to show up, time and time again.

49

"Legal Eze"

A Tale of Small Town Justice

When Clarence "Easy" Easterling opened his law practice in the old bank building on Broad Street, folks thought his Harvard degree would make him too highfalutin for small-town Georgia justice. What they didn't expect was how he'd translate big-city law into front-porch wisdom.

"Legal ease ain't the same as Legal Eze," he'd say, making sure even the most tongue-tied farmer could understand their rights. "The law's like creek water—looks complicated when it's rushing by, but it's clear as day when you take time to let it settle."

His secretary, Miss Betsy, who'd worked for three generations of lawyers, would smile when clients came in worried about affidavits and jurisdictions, only to leave understanding their situation as clearly as Sunday's sermon. "Mr. Easy," she'd say, "has a way of turning legal molasses into sweet tea."

Even Judge Harrison, known for his strict adherence to protocol, had to admit that Easy's folksy translations of complex statutes often did more justice than any leather-bound law book.

Justice's Translation

Charles E. Cravey

Where legal terms meet Southern ways,

Through courthouse halls and judgment days,

Some lawyers find that simple truth

Serves better than their formal youth.

Past Latin phrases, stern and strong,

Through words that help folks get along,

The law finds voice in common ground.

Where wisdom makes a clearer sound.

For some speak high and some speak low,

While others help the meaning flow—

Like creek water, clean and bright,

Making murky laws turn right.

Reflection on Simple Justice

In the South, we understand that true wisdom isn't about showing what you know—it's about helping others understand. We know that justice works best when it speaks the language of the people it serves, when it flows as naturally as front porch conversation.

These courthouse moments teach us that sometimes the most powerful legal argument is the one that speaks to the heart as well as the mind, which translates complexity into clarity without losing its meaning.

Because some lawyers don't just practice law—they make it make sense. They bridge the gap between legal jargon and everyday life, ensuring that justice is accessible to everyone, not just those with the privilege of higher education. In this small town, where magnolia trees line the streets and everyone knows your name, the law becomes a living, breathing entity—part of the community tapestry, woven into the very essence of daily life.

Easy Easterling's approach is a reminder that empathy and understanding are just as crucial in the legal profession as any statute or regulation. His practice isn't merely about winning cases; it's about fostering trust and respect, about making sure that justice isn't just seen to be done but truly understood and felt by all.

In a world that often feels overwhelming and complex, there's a certain beauty in simplicity, a strength in clarity, and a profound impact in making sure every voice is heard and every story is told. Here, in this corner of Georgia, law and life intertwine seamlessly, proving that when justice is served with a touch of grace and a dose of humanity, it truly serves all.

50

At the Heart of Southern Stories

A Final Reflection

In the South, stories aren't just told—they're savored, like the last spoonful of peach cobbler at a Sunday dinner. They rise with the morning mist over mountain hollows, drift through courthouse squares where ancient oaks stand sentinel, and settle soft as evening dew on front porch rockers where tales have been passed down through generations.

Our stories live in the spaces between words, in the knowing glances exchanged over sweet tea, in the gentle "bless your hearts" that can mean a thousand different things. They're carried on the wind through cotton fields and down red clay roads, whispered by river waters and sung by whip-poor-wills in the gloaming hour.

We tell them in layers, like the strata of soil beneath our feet—rich, complex, sometimes uncomfortable, but always honest about who we are and where we've been. Every small town has its keeper of tales, every family its historian, every courthouse its archive of human nature laid bare in testimonies and treaties, marriages, and deeds.

These aren't just stories about place—though Lord knows our connection to the land runs deeper than kudzu roots. They're not just stories about people—though every character is as real as the humidity in August.

They're stories about time itself, about how the past lives on in present moments, and about how tomorrow is born from yesterday's dreams.

In the South, we understand that a good story, like a good biscuit, takes time to rise properly. It needs the warmth of human connection, the proper measure of truth and grace, and just enough salt to bring out the flavor of life. Our tales might meander like a lowland river, taking their sweet time to reach the point, but that's because we know the journey matters as much as the destination.

We tell stories to remember who we are, to understand who we're becoming, and to pass along the wisdom that can't be taught any other way. They're our inheritance and our legacy, as vital as the recipes handed down on flour-dusted index cards and as valuable as the family Bible with its recorded births and deaths.

Whether they're told across worn wooden counters in country stores, shared over back fences between neighbors, or whispered in twilight to wide-eyed children, our stories hold the heart of who we are. They remind us that grace can appear in the most unexpected places, that redemption often wears overalls, and that sometimes the most powerful truths come wrapped in the simplest packages.

Because at the heart of every Southern story—whether it's about a grand old Victorian keeping watch over a changing town, a river that holds centuries in its depths, or a farmer reading wisdom in rows of corn—there's a deeper truth about what it means to be human, to belong to a place and a people, to hold on and to let go, to endure and to grow.

These stories are our way of saying, This is who we are. This is what we value. This is what we hope to be. They're our love letters to a way of life that values front porch conversations over social media posts, that measures wealth in relationships rather than dollars, that understands tomorrow's promises often depend on yesterday's wisdom.

And so we keep telling them these stories of our South—not just to preserve the past, but to light the way forward, to remind ourselves and our children that in a world of constant change, some things are worth holding onto: dignity, grace, courage, and the ability to find beauty in the ordinary moments that make up an extraordinary life.

Because in the end, that's what lies at the heart of every Southern story—the extraordinary truth hiding in plain sight, waiting to be discovered by those who take the time to listen, to understand, and to pass it along.

Other Books by Dr. Charles E. Cravey may be Found at:

https://drcharlescravey.com or

Amazon.com/charles cravey books